HOW i LEARNED
ENGLiSH

ALSO BY TOM MILLER

The Panama Hat Trail
On the Border
Trading with the Enemy: A Yankee Travels through Castro's Cuba
Jack Ruby's Kitchen Sink
The Assassination Please Almanac
The Interstate Gourmet: Texas and the Southwest (coauthor)
Writing on the Edge: A Borderlands Reader (ed.)
Travelers' Tales—Cuba (ed.)
Arizona: The Land and the People (ed.)

55 ACCOMPLiSHED LATiNOS RECALL LESSONS iN LANGUAGE AND LiFE

HOW i LEARNED ENGLiSH

EDiTED BY TOM MiLLER

NATIONAL GEOGRAPHIC

WASHINGTON, D.C.

Published by the National Geographic Society
Copyright © 2007 Tom Miller.
All rights reserved. Reproduction of the whole or any part of the contents without written permission
from the publisher is prohibited.

Copyrights and permissions can be found on pages 266–67.

ISBN: 978-1-4262-0097-7

Library of Congress Cataloging-in-Publication Data available upon request

Founded in 1888, the National Geographic Society is one of the largest nonprofit scientific and
educational organizations in the world. It reaches more than 285 million people worldwide each
month through its official journal, NATIONAL GEOGRAPHIC, and its four other magazines; the
National Geographic Channel; television documentaries; radio programs; films; books; videos
and DVDs; maps; and interactive media. National Geographic has funded more than 8,000
scientific research projects and supports an education program combating geographic illiteracy.

For more information, please call 1-800-NGS LINE (647-5463) or write to the following address:

NATIONAL GEOGRAPHIC SOCIETY
1145 17th Street N.W.
Washington, DC 20036-4688 U.S.A.

Visit us online at www.nationalgeographic.com/books

For information about special discounts for bulk purchases, please contact National Geographic
Books Special Sales: ngspecsales@ngs.org.

Printed in the U.S.A.

Interior Design: Melissa Farris

CONTENTS

To the memory of my Baltic ancestors and the future of my Caribbean family

To tell you the truth, the hardest thing about coming to this country wasn't the winter everyone warned me about—it was the language.... For the longest time I thought Americans must be smarter than us Latins—because how else could they speak such a difficult language. After a while, it struck me the other way. Given the choice of languages, only a fool would choose to speak English on purpose.

—from *¡Yo!*, by Julia Alvarez

FOREWORD

— RAY SUAREZ —

THIS BOOK REACHES your hands at a peculiar time in the life of the United States. Language is no longer just a way to communicate with others, to put muscle and flesh onto thoughts and feelings. No, language has become a battleground, as one group of Americans challenges another's legitimate claim to fully vested ownership of a shared identity.

How I Learned English is a product of a newer kind of immigration, and a newer attitude toward language. There was no *How I Learned English* for Italian-Americans in the 1940s. There was no *How I Learned English* for German-Americans in the 1870s. There is something different afoot. And it's not making everybody happy.

Samuel Huntington, writing in *Foreign Policy* magazine, looks at Latino America and totally misses the night school classes, the endless hours of ads for English-language home study kits, and the struggles and victories of the people in this book. In "Jose, Can You See?" he peers into the future and sees native-born English-speakers as an embattled minority, increasingly marginalized in their own country. "Because most of those whose first language is Spanish will also probably have some fluency in English," Huntington explains, "English speakers lacking fluency in Spanish are likely to be and feel at a disadvantage in the competition for jobs, promotions, and contracts."

How do you say "Trick Bag" in Spanish?

Begin learning the language once you arrive, and at some point you will be told Spanish speakers are not interested in acquiring the language, and even if they're interested, they're not learning it fast enough. Learn the language, and you may end up oppressing your monolingual neighbors because of their mastery of just one tongue.

If you do not demand logic and coherence from these debates about language, you will not be disappointed. Unlike riding a bicycle, ice-skating, or typing, language acquisition involves much more than simple mastery of a skill. As you will see in the pages of this collection, learning a language begins a passage to another way of seeing the world and speaking it into existence. For many of the essayists, embarking on a new journey with English was really the beginning of an encounter, a relationship, a maddening and rewarding wrestling match that, for some, continues decades later.

As American culture reached the remotest corners of the Earth in the decades after World War II, a kind of mass seduction also began. In Asia, Africa, Eastern Europe, and Latin America, I have met people of all ages and circumstances who are attracted, repelled, and fascinated by the very idea of America, an idea that is transmitted in English. The power of English is asserted in every corner of the globe, from nonsensical slogans on the T-shirts of Japanese teenagers (Happy Teen Force Patrol?) to pop songs sung phonetically—uncomprehended—on an Eastern European street corner to the request of a shy Cuban to spend a few minutes practicing the language of Uncle Sam.

The power of English often comes with ambivalence. Along with the access to a wider world that English provides comes hesitation about having to join the club. I don't mean the kind of feeling that causes Americans to ask, "Why do they hate us?" as much as the one that causes people elsewhere to ask themselves, "Is it OK to love them?"

For many of the writers who follow in these pages, the need to learn English was accompanied by wrenching personal circumstances: exile, illness, economic migration, family dissolution. So language was just another challenge for people already up to their young chins in sudden change. For others, it was a proffered ticket to a new kind of membership in the modern and changing world. Along with wrapping your mouth around those hard consonants and struggling to master those bedeviling "exceptions to the rules" came the promise of an exciting adventure. You can almost taste, touch, and smell the anticipation in the memories of the gifted storytellers that follow.

In the 1980s I once interviewed a community activist in Chicago who was raised in an orphanage after the death of his parents when he was barely out of diapers. "They stole my tongue," he told me. "They saved my life, but I lost Spanish in the process." The rueful tone accompanying his life story was striking. Now in his 50s, he could barely remember his parents at all, but the loss of Spanish was palpable for him even now.

How different is that from the regrets of hundreds of thousands of other children of immigrants who grew up with that old ethic, "English above all, the faster the better, and you'll be able to put away your old life even faster"?

That delicate dance between mastery and loss is very much with us in the stories in this book. It can be seen in the young strivers who work in every spare moment to conquer English, in the children who refuse to speak Spanish to their parents, and in the parents who struggle to speak English to their children. In the end, the questions remain: How American am I going to be? Will I still be that other thing—Puerto Rican, Mexican, Cuban, Peruvian, Honduran?

We may be setting aside that old argument about assimilation. As one Mexican who came to the United States once asked me, "Why would it be good to become less than I am to become an American? I have taken on this new thing, English, but that doesn't mean I have to put away who I was when I got here."

The writers in the coming pages tell hilarious stories. They tell sad stories. They tell of wanting to fit in, of desperation to succeed, and of a steady march toward making it in a new society. Sometimes that journey is taken by a family facing similar trials of school, workplace, and the street. For many others, a solo journey starts in the Spanish-speaking world and becomes a voyage of transformation for a nervy adventurer who, by the way, learns English in the process.

Many of the writers, performers, and scholars you are about to read are people I have known as interview subjects and as friends, or whom I have admired from afar for their achievement, skill, and creativity. In their various stories, they tell you something about the millions of Americans whose first language is Spanish or Portuguese. Many now look back on their experiences and see that they are rooted in two places. That's important.

During the ferocious debates to come over the fraternal twins of language and immigration, you will see many native-born and monolingual people fret over the loss of the country they grew up with. It certainly seems to scare the hell out of Samuel Huntington. The transformative power of both America and English acquisition, power that shouts from the pages of this book, is forgotten. That power is lost in the wailing over the coming bilingual dystopia.

Those handwringers might take comfort from this book. In hundreds of pages, there is hardly an inkling that learning English regardless all the craziness on the way there, is not a very desirable skill.

Sure, there are stories of loneliness and isolation that immigrants from anywhere will certainly understand and remember. And sure, there are the petty slights newcomers have faced since the earliest of cross-cultural migrations. There are sad miscommunications right along with the hilarious ones.

Maybe you learned English yourself. Maybe you are struggling to turn those half-remembered phrases from high school Spanish into something more like a functioning language. Either way, you will recognize yourself somewhere in these pages.

Ray Suarez is senior correspondent for *The NewsHour with Jim Lehrer* on PBS.

INTRODUCTION

— TOM MILLER —

JUST THIS MORNING, a front-page story told of the enormous demand throughout the United States for courses in English as a Second Language (ESL). Immigrants, regardless of their economic, legal, or employment status, know that speaking English increases their potential at work and play. Learning a language as a youngster is easier than as an adult. At any age it can be grueling, painful, aggravating, fulfilling, amusing, instructive, gratifying, and rewarding—sometimes all of these, sometimes all at once.

When my wife came home from her first day in ESL class, I asked what she had learned. "Oh, really?" Regla replied. "That's interesting." Her first four words in English showed polite curiosity and superficial nicety. In fact, to everything I asked, she responded, "Oh, really? That's interesting." What was the teacher like? "Oh, really? That's interesting." Were there many other students? "Oh, really? That's interesting." Did you break for lunch? "Oh, really? That's interesting." Over the years it's become a running gag.

Regla's first ESL class took place at a neighborhood community center that offered free courses as a public service. Her fellow students were mainly the wives of day laborers and of recently arrived *campesinos.* She next took a semester at a university ESL center, where her classmates were doctors, physicists, engineers, economists, and chemists—not the image of typical ESL students, but just as anxious to learn a new language. Finally she completed her ESL studies at a community college.

Early on in this country's history, local schools often offered instruction in the language of its main immigrant student population combined, frequently, with English. States passed English instruction laws toward the end of the 19th century, only to repeal them not long after. Some cities, though, did away with bilingual classes altogether and relegated foreign languages to high school instruction only.

When waves of Italian and Eastern European immigrants arrived in the early 1900s, philanthropists underwrote night school English classes, notes James Crawford, an authority on bilingual education, "while indoctrinating immigrants in 'free enterprise' values." Industrialists such as Henry Ford insisted his employees attend loyalty classes, and "an ideological link was forged between language and 'Americanism.'" After the Spanish-American War, an effort to force public schools on the newly acquired island of Puerto Rico to teach only in English was so disastrous that soon the attempt at linguistic colonization was diluted and eventually, after World War II, abandoned.

"We have room for but one language in this country," Theodore Roosevelt wrote ten years after he left the presidency, "and that is the English language, for we intend to see that the crucible turns out people as Americans…and not as dwellers in a polyglot boarding house." Roosevelt pushed for more classes for immigrants to learn English, but also "the deportation of those who failed to do so within five years." This attitude got a boost in Nebraska, where, in 1919, the legislature passed a statute that English "become the mother tongue of all children reared in this state." (The U.S. Supreme Court overturned that law four years later in *Meyer v. Nebraska*.)

There isn't just one way to learn English, as the contributors to this collection prove. Most of them built their English on a foundation of Spanish (or Portuguese). And most of the immigrants who tackle English today start with this underpinning. Just 75 years ago, though, the source of most immigration was European. In *The Education of H*Y*M*A*N K*A*P*L*A*N*, a droll 1937 entertainment by Leonard Q. Ross, all the students at New York's American Night Preparatory School for Adults came from Germany or Poland. Ross, the pen name of Polish immigrant Leo Rosten, author of *The Joys of Yiddish*, wrote of one student whose remarkable contortions of the English language constantly bewildered his exasperated teacher Mr. Parkhill. The beguiling and innocent Mr. Kaplan, who always signed his name with asterisks between capital letters, told the class that the plural of blouse was blice, of sandwich was delicatessen, and that among United States presidents were Judge Vashington, James Medicine, and Abram Lincohen.

Upper-class foreigners, in the days when working-class Hyman Kaplan took courses, were taught through a new approach called English as a Second Language. By the 1950s, ESL had spread to all levels to combat "cultural deprivation" and "language disability," as one account had it.

My own upbringing was entirely in English, surrounded by wall-to-wall books and a surfeit of daily newspapers. When my parents didn't want us to understand them, they spoke household Yiddish. In the late 1960s I moved to the American Southwest, and over the years have often traveled from there into Latin America. In both places, I have met innumerable people for whom English was a second language and have become intrigued with how they acquired this new way of speaking and how it affected their lives. Increasingly my personal and professional friendships developed with those for whom English was not native, as mine was, but another layer. Finally, I married into a Spanish-speaking family and watched in admiration as first my wife, and then my stepsons, learned American English and adapted to its cultural foibles, inexplicable idioms, and linguistic idiosyncrasies.

The contributors to this book are neither culturally deprived nor linguistically disabled. On the contrary, they each have something to contribute to the English-speaking world. Many speak more than two languages. I've always thought that speaking a second language could make you more mentally agile but not necessarily smarter. I've known plenty of people whose lingual was more semi than bi.

Yet by the time someone adds a third language to the mix they're either on the ball or on the run.

The killer in English, as in all languages, is the preposition. Nowhere did this strike me more than in Manhattan, where Regla and I once sublet a fifth-floor apartment in a heavily Dominican neighborhood near 145th Street and Broadway. The building super, whose apartment was situated next to the elevator in the lobby, had posted a sign on his front door, with an American flag near the top. THANK YOU, AMERICA, it read, FOR ALL THAT YOU HAVE DONE TO US. Was ever a preposition so artfully misconstrued?

I rather like the notion of Theodore Roosevelt's polyglot boardinghouse and would be happy to lodge there. I suspect many of this book's contributors would stay there as well. In fact, we may have already done that, dear reader, and what follows just may be a transcript of our multilingual arguments and pontifications going deep into the night. Now *that's* interesting.

ACKNOWLEDGMENTS

IF SOMEONE ASKED YOU to suggest a friend whose first language was Spanish or Portuguese and whose second (or third or fourth) language is English, whom would you recommend? I asked dozens of friends and colleagues that very question when I undertook this book and came up with three times more names than you'll find in the table of contents. The list winnowed itself down to a manageable size due to availability, deadline, and accessibility. To reach many of the writers in the following pages, generous people intervened on my behalf or allowed me a peek at their Rolodexes. To them I am grateful for their recommendations and their assistance. (A few who suggested others were already participants themselves. Takes one to know one.) These helpful people are: David Unger, Eliana Rivero, Rubén Martínez, Lucinda Zoe, Peter Young, Nancy Hand, Susan Bergholz, Stuart Bernstein, Gloria Gutiérrez, Ingrid Lopet, Brian O'Gara, Hugo Pérez, Steve Larson, Pablo Medina, Mark Weiss, Carlos Morton, Demetria Martínez, Jordan Levin, Felipe Gallardo, Lourdes García-Navarro, Esther Allen, and Enrique Fernández.

I am particularly indebted to the following for noteworthy help and advice beyond the call: Gary Kenton, Eliane Rubinstein-Avila, Jesús Vega, Gay Salisbury, the late Ricardo Aguilar, Charles Miller, and Kelley Merriam Castro. I take perverse pride in keeping my knowledge of computer functions to a minimum, but certain skills unknown to me were required at a moment's notice. Mark Bryant dropped in when called, and Wynne Rife tinkered with my Web site when needed. My editor at National Geographic Books, Elizabeth Newhouse, understood this book's potential from the day I casually described the idea to her. Finally, compiling contributions and permissions from dozens of sources and various literary agents, advising on a spreadsheet, and assembling an unwieldy manuscript complete with biographies and other floating material was something beyond my patience and ability. Annamarie Schaecher, a graduate student in Mexican American Studies at the University of Arizona, took on the task and barreled through the whole process knowledgably and admirably. To all of you trusted colleagues, my heartfelt appreciation in the language of your choice.

part one

*The Hatter's remark seemed to her
to have no sort of meaning to it,
and yet it was certainly English.*

—Alice, at the Mad Tea Party,
from *Alice's Adventures in Wonderland*
by Lewis Carroll

Learning English with Shotaro

— RUTH BEHAR —

I HAVE SPOKEN ENGLISH for more than 40 years and I still haven't forgotten that English is not my first language. Even now I hesitate as I put down this first sentence. Does it sound right in English? Is it stilted? Is it correct to say "I have" and "haven't" and "is not" in the same sentence? I honestly don't, do not, know.

It's strange, and maybe even absurd, that I should feel this way. I speak English perfectly. I wrote my Ph.D. thesis in English. I think, dream, and live much of my life in the English language. "You're from Cuba?" people say, surprised. "But you don't have an accent." No, I don't have an accent, though as a teenager I tried hard to imitate a British accent, because I thought it was more refined than the accent I heard around me growing up in Queens, New York. I spoke to my parents only in Spanish, as I do even today, because that is the language in which they're most comfortable.

Mami and Papi definitely have an accent, a thick Cuban accent, when they speak English, and I continue to correct their grammatical and pronunciation mistakes, as I started to do as a child. For me English was always the public language, the language of power, competition, and progress, and also the language of solitude, the language where I was totally on my own, without my parents to help me. Now I speak an English that can't be recognized as being from anywhere specific. My younger brother, years ago, put it exactly right. He said what I have is a "college accent." It's the English of a person who went to school, studied hard, and got good grades because she feared if she didn't she'd be sent back to the dumb class.

No one can tell by looking at me or hearing me speak that another language burns inside me, an invisible but eternal flame. No one can tell I came to the English language the way a woman in another era came to her husband in an arranged marriage—trying to make the best of a relationship someone else chose for her and hoping one day she would fall in love. I'm still waiting… I depend on English, I'm grateful I speak English, I wouldn't be anyone if I didn't know English. But I'm not in love with English.

My mother tongue is Spanish. This is the language I spoke as a little girl in Cuba for the first four and a half years of my life. I am told I spoke that little girl's Spanish with a lot of spunk. They tell me I was a nonstop talker, *una cotorrita*. But after we arrived in the United States I became shy, silent, sullen. I have no memory of myself as a little girl speaking Spanish in Cuba. I guess that's why every time I'm in Cuba and I see a little girl letting Spanish roll off her tongue so naturally, so effortlessly, my heart melts. "That was me!" I think. That was me, once upon a time, before I became self-conscious about which *lengua* I was speaking. I go to Cuba as an anthropologist, the way I also go to Spain and Mexico and Argentina, continually seeking opportunities to listen to Spanish and to speak Spanish, and in those countries I can't help but imitate their accents, so that my Spanish is a hodgepodge, the Spanish of a woman who no longer knows where her home is.

When we left Cuba after the revolution, we went to Israel, and I am told I became fluent in Hebrew. I might have already known a few words, because in Havana I attended kindergarten at the Centro Israelita, a bilingual Spanish-Yiddish day school founded by Jewish immigrants who settled in Cuba in the 1920s and 1930s. But Hebrew didn't stick in our family, because after a year we left Israel for New York and we never spoke it at home. Hebrew was the language of the liturgy and it lost for us its connection to everyday life. Spanish became our home language, and I spoke it with my grandparents, not only my Ladino-speaking grandparents from Turkey but also my Yiddish-speaking grandparents from Poland and Russia.

So before the age of five I spoke two languages, Spanish and Hebrew, and then I was dropped into a first-grade classroom at P.S. 117 in Queens, where I was expected to somehow survive even though I was unable to utter a word of English. This was in 1962, before bilingual programs and English as a Second Language were introduced into the public school system. You sank or you swam. You learned English by osmosis, ear training, lip reading, like a baby, without any special instruction and not a drop of mercy. Or you failed to learn English and you entered the dumb class and stayed there forever.

In that first-grade classroom, I vividly recall the teacher, Mrs. Sarota, writing a math problem on the blackboard. I knew the answer and I raised my hand. Mrs. Sarota smiled and nodded, raised her eyebrows, and waited, chalk in hand. I opened my mouth, but no words came out. I knew the answer, but I didn't know how to say it in English. I sat there mutely. "Ruth," the teacher said. "Do you know the answer or not?" I wasn't accustomed to hearing my name spoken in English. It sounded harsh. Ugly. In my family, I'm called "Ruti," and the two syllables are said slowly, languorously.

"Well, Ruth?" The teacher said my name like an insult. I attempted sign language, trying to write the answer in the air with my fingers. Soon the other children were giggling and pointing at me, as though I were a monkey escaped from the zoo. I felt so ashamed, I lowered my head and pretended to disappear. I retreated into silence for the rest of the school year.

By second grade I was in the dumb class and I definitely felt I deserved to be there. Although the school claimed not to make any distinctions, as kids we knew that for each grade there was a dumb class made up of children who'd flunked out the previous year. To be in the dumb class in second grade was a sure sign you'd gotten off to a terrible start in life, because things had to be pretty bad for a kid to flunk first grade. The teacher acted as if we were not only dumb but deaf, and she repeated things and stood over us, watching as we wrote in our notebooks, ready to pounce on our mistakes. Some of the kids in the class were slow learners, but a few were retarded, like Grace, who had a huge head and wore shoes several sizes too large and was so friendly that you knew something had to be wrong with her. In those days, the dumb class was also where they put the foreign kids until they could speak and prove to the world they were actually smart and just needed to learn English—or until they revealed that deep down they really *were* dumb.

Fortunately I wasn't alone in the dumb class. Shotaro, a boy from Japan, was also in the dumb class because he spoke a language that wasn't English. As the only two foreign kids, we became close friends. We looked at picture books together and read to one another and played tag and hopscotch during recess. He was the only boy I invited to my birthday party in second grade. One of the pictures I most recall from those years is the Polaroid of a group of girls posed around the M&M-studded cake, me and Shotaro in the middle beaming from the sheer joy of standing next to each other. I think we learned to speak English to be able to communicate with one another, though there was an understanding between us which was mysterious and deep and went beyond words.

We both did well and got good at English. By the end of the school year we were both released from the dumb class and assigned to a regular third-grade class. But Shotaro and I didn't continue together in third grade. His family decided to return to Japan, while for my family, it had become clear, there was not going to be any return to Cuba.

I was sad to see Shotaro go. He gave me a going-away present that I still store at my parents' house with other keepsakes from my childhood. It was a pair of miniature wooden male and female dolls, outfitted in matching kimonos and nested together in a silk brocade box. Maybe the dolls were intended to represent the two of us, a girl and a boy, who grew into the English language together during a year spent in the dumb class. Neither of us spoke the other's language, so English was our common tongue—English and a faith that we were not dumb, that what we were was dispossessed.

University of Michigan anthropology professor **RUTH BEHAR** (Havana, Cuba; 1956-) has won a MacArthur "genius award" and a Guggenheim Fellowship. Her books include *Translated Woman: Crossing the Border with Esperanza's Story* and *The Vulnerable Observer: Anthropology That Breaks Your Heart.* Her newest title is *An Island Called Home: Returning to Jewish Cuba.*

Mississippi, Girdles, and John Wooden

– GABRIEL ROZMAN –

MY FIRST LANGUAGE was Hungarian, even though I was born in Uruguay. My parents and a large family contingent were trying to get away from the war in Europe to a safer place like South America. I say this because after speaking a language as complex as Hungarian, one loses the fear of learning other languages. As a matter of fact, as I look back at my decision at age 20 in 1961 to study in the United States at the university level, I still do not understand what drove me to believe that I could interact in English with the level of knowledge I had of the language.

My college destination in the United States was no less than Hattiesburg, Mississippi—the only place that would take me starting my school year on January 1 since I had missed all the other application deadlines. In 1961, believe me, all the English I had learned in high school had nothing to do with the language I encountered upon my arrival in Mississippi. I told myself that I had wasted my time trying to learn an English nobody around me spoke.

A few months later I transferred to California State University in Los Angeles. Since I needed to work to support myself, I applied for a position with Sears in Hollywood. They gave me a test that consisted of a series of numbers, figures, and analytical questions. Since I scored higher on the test than the other applicants, I was allowed to choose which position within the store I wanted. Of course, I asked which paid the most! I was told sales, in the catalog department.

I accepted.

Here we have a bit of a mismatch. My English vocabulary was in the hundreds of words and the Sears Catalog had 200,000 items. But at age 21 there is no challenge that seems too big. I took the catalog home and read for hours, trying to memorize the names of the items. I got through only a few hundred, so I designed a strategy: if I did not know the item a customer asked about, I would pose a few general questions until I figured out what they wanted. Then I'd look in the approximate pages of the catalog until the person would point it out to me.

When the store opened the next morning, the first person to approach me was an old lady (at least from the prospective of a 21-year-old). She said she wanted to purchase a "girdle." I had no idea what she was talking about, but—being so smart—I asked what this girdle could be used for! The lady turned red and left, and my manager then started teaching me a bit more English.

A month later at a business law class in college, we were getting back the grades from the midterm test. I got an A. One of the other students—a native Californian—got a C. He got up in class to complain about his grade, telling the professor that he knew the material and was unfairly graded because he had difficulties expressing the points of law in good English. The professor looked at him, came to where I was sitting and picked up my test, and showing it to him, said: "Here is a student who can hardly talk intelligently; he writes like an eight-year-old; his calligraphy is terrible and all his verbs are in the present tense. Nevertheless he correctly answered the test." I looked around the class to understand from the faces of my fellow students whether I should be offended by the facts expressed or smile as I was being complimented.

I look at the way we studied languages 40 years ago and marvel that we were able to learn enough even to survive asking for a meal. I watch today as people study multiple languages using the Internet, videos, interactive software, audiotapes, and other great tools and ask myself why every young person is not studying at least one more language. Without English I would never have been able to enjoy Mississippi (well, just about) or eventually get an MBA at UCLA at the time John Wooden was the basketball coach and the UCLA team was unbeatable.

GABRIEL ROZMAN (Montevideo, Uruguay; 1941-) holds a business degree from California State University and an MBA from UCLA. Currently he is president of TCS Iberoamerica, a multinational company that handles systems development, technology, and software development for corporations throughout the Americas, Spain, and Portugal.

Trilingual Ease

— FRANC J. CAMARA —

COMING TO THE UNITED STATES was one of the most exciting events of my life. I never took the experience itself as a challenge, though, but rather as an adventure and a life-changing opportunity.

I grew up in a small Mayan village in the state of Yucatán in Mexico, where the vast majority of the people spoke Maya. In fact, to this day, many people there still speak Maya as their primary language, and some as their only language.

While growing up, my parents, their siblings, their parents, and most everyone around me spoke Maya whenever they talked to one another. However, because of a government mandate for Spanish to be the recognized official language, Maya was discouraged. Some of us were forced to speak only Spanish.

Our teachers punished Maya-only-speaking children whenever they said something in our native language. I remember vividly, in grade school, when a teacher hit a student with a stick for speaking Maya in class. We were told, over and over, that speaking Maya was bad, and that it would never get us anywhere. My fourth-grade teacher told us that if we wanted to grow up to be somebody, that we needed to learn Spanish well and to forget Maya since it was worthless. (With the same attitude, he once told me that only uneducated and dirty people whistle.) On the other hand, if we wanted to be only peasants or blue-collar workers, then we should continue to speak Maya—but, under no circumstance, think about speaking it in his class. His job was to educate people that deserved to be educated.

Because of this blatant oppression of Maya-speaking people, my parents were adamant about speaking Spanish to me and my siblings. They fought hard to make sure we spoke only Spanish among ourselves even if it was all broken and grammatically incorrect. Still, it was almost impossible for us not to learn or speak Maya. Wherever we went, if we wanted to talk to others, we needed, at minimum, to understand what they were saying. The "elite" were the only ones that didn't have to speak Maya, because they lived in a "different" world. They dined well and had cars and servants. We had nothing to speak of. In fact, there were times when we didn't have anything to eat. In my hometown, we were separated by social status; as a result, there was no getting away from the Mayan language.

Aside from encouraging us not to speak Maya within the family, my mother made it a point for us to understand the value of education. She always said that if we wanted to get ahead in life, education would be the door—the "way in." Neither she nor my father had gone to school. They were both illiterate. In fact, my mother didn't even learn to sign her name until my sister and I taught her how to do it. That was the extent of her writing abilities. My father, on the other hand, taught himself how to read and write Spanish, and even did the same with English. His grammar may not be the best, but he did learn enough to get by.

At the age of 15, after finishing junior high school in my hometown, I convinced my father to help me come to the States. He had already lived there for years. My goal was to study electronics in depth. I had already finished a mail-order electronics course in Mexico. After my studies, I would go back to my hometown to grow my shop.

My father tried to register me at a technical trade school even before I arrived in Los Angeles, but I was too young, didn't speak English, and didn't have a GED. The school's guidance counselor recommended that I learn English, go to high school, and then come back. As a result, when I arrived, my father enrolled me in an intensive English school, which gave me a student visa.

I attended that school seven hours a day, Monday through Friday. The school offered two classes daily—one in the morning that focused on grammar, and the other in the afternoon that concentrated on conversation. Each "level" was four weeks long. The entire course was made up of seven levels ranging from a very basic introduction all the way to writing essays, advanced reading, and poetry.

Living in Los Angeles was a challenge. Surrounded by gangs, drug deals, and crime in general, most people around me spoke Spanish, so there wasn't even a chance to practice the English I was learning. As a result, I decided to hang out with my classmates, many of whom were businesspeople from countries throughout the world. Even though we knew very little English, we had no choice but to practice the little we had learned with each other. The rest of the time, we used body language to communicate.

Most of the classmates that I spent time with were from Japan, so I learned about their food, how to use chopsticks properly, their traditions, and even some of their language. One of my classmates has been a great friend ever since. When he lived in Japan years later, I visited him every time I went to Tokyo. He now lives with his family in the Philippines, where he owns a hotel. I've visited him a couple of times in the last few years.

To further practice English while learning it, I made it a point to watch only English-language television. In particular, I enjoyed comedies, which taught me a lot about the American culture. *Three's Company* was one of my favorites. At first, I didn't understand what was going on, but as time went by, I actually caught myself laughing at their innuendos.

To train my ears further, I loved listening to music, writing down the lyrics, and singing along with the radio. I used a headset to make sure I caught as much detail as possible. In fact, that's how I studied everyday—with my music blasting while doing homework and singing at the same time. Duran Duran, Van Halen, and U2 helped me learn English.

For most foreigners, pronunciation is usually the biggest challenge. To make sure mine was the best possible, I used to watch how English-speaking people moved their lips when they spoke, and imitated them while looking at myself in a mirror.

To further test my vocabulary and hearing skills, I'd listen to AM talk radio and *Mystery Theatre*. For the latter, I wrote down my own clues and conclusions to see whether I understood what was going on. To work on my accent, I recorded myself reading stories and listened for mistakes. I did this over and over, and even practiced dictation from my own recording.

These exercises and others, like reading everything in sight–signs, graffiti, and fliers, for example–helped me learn English fast and, most of all, as well as possible. As a result, I finished the entire intensive English course on time and with honors.

From there, I went to high school where, because of the short time I had been in the States, nobody could believe that I spoke and understood English as well as I did. Further, because I had not transferred from an American junior high school, according to Board of Education rules I was not allowed to go into "regular" classes–or so I was told. I insisted so much that they placed me in the highest possible level of the English as a Second Language program. The teacher was so impressed with my skills that she requested I take a test and be placed in regular English classes.

At the time, it was obvious to me that students who had transferred from foreign schools were immediately labeled as "below average," and quite possibly as "dumb." In fact, in Mexico, I had already taken algebra and even an introduction to calculus. Because I was a foreign student, though, I was placed in basic math. That drove me nuts! I was being "taught" how to add and subtract when I should have been working on advanced equations. Once again, within a matter of months, I challenged the class and moved to higher math.

By the time I finished high school, I was in Advanced Placement English competing with native English speakers. At the same school, I majored in math and computer science while instructing teachers how to program a computer after learning from reading programming books I took out of the public library and "running" my programs in my head.

Not only did I finish high school in five semesters instead of six, I was also the valedictorian, which I considered a major achievement for someone who had been in the States only three years and had started from not knowing a single word of English.

As a child, I was told that Spanish was the language that was going to forge me ahead in Mexico, instead of Maya. Soon after I arrived in the United States, I realized that learning English well, immersing myself in the American culture, and continuing my education was the right combination and the key to success.

Back in my Mexican hometown, many people believe that Maya speakers can learn English more easily than those who do not speak Maya. In fact, now that speaking Maya is "hip," due to the global interest in Mayan culture, those who looked down upon the Maya-speaking people are now wishing they had learned it as children.

Personally, I don't think it's about speaking Maya, but rather about being exposed to more than one language at an early age. Albeit a blessing for me, my multilingual ability was ironically developed by fear and oppression, but instead of looking at it that way, I've learned to leverage it and use it as a foundation for my success. In fact, in college, instead of taking Spanish (as the required foreign language), I took French, which ended up being my minor. Further into my career, I even learned enough Japanese to use while traveling alone in Japan.

Of course, my first passion is technology, but my second is languages. In my view, languages open the door to the world, present us with a wealth of opportunities, and open our minds to countless experiences. Having traveled to around 30 countries, I can personally attest to that.

A multilingual computer scientist, **FRANC J. CAMARA** (Oxkutzcab, Mexico; 1964-) holds an MBA from California Lutheran

University. Camara worked at Microsoft from 1993 to 2005, rising to director of Worldwide Small & Medium Business Competitive Product Strategies. Now a consultant to the computer industry, Camara gives motivational talks to Latino audiences and has been active in the Society of Hispanic MBAs and civic groups in Washington State.

Power

— MARIE ARANA —

Excerpted from *American Chica: Two Worlds, One Childhood*

THE PLAYGROUND OF THE ROOSEVELT SCHOOL was swarming with hundreds of children, milling about and yammering, waiting for the bell to ring. We edged through the gate and stood in awe.

A girl about my age leaned against the wall and stared at us. She was dark-skinned, frail, her eyes bulging from her face like boiled eggs, blue-white and rubbery.

"*Primer día?*" she asked. First day? I was gawking around me, an obvious newcomer. I nodded that it was so.

"You speak English," she said, more of a fact than a question.

"Yes," I answered, ready to prove it. But she continued in Spanish, and my affirmation hung in the air like a hiss.

"Then you'll be fine," she assured me. "Don't look so worried. I'm Margarita Martínez. My English is not so good. They put me in Señora Arellano's class."

There were two streams for every grade at Roosevelt, Margarita explained. The main one was for English speakers, a smaller one for those who spoke better Spanish. I would be tested for my abilities and streamed according to my tongue.

The man who would decide my fortune was vexed in the company of children. I could see it the moment he called out my name. He was frowning and fidgety, flicking his hair with his fingers and peering impatiently at his wrist.

I followed his orange head into a room next to the headmaster's office.

"Do you speak English or Spanish at home, señorita?" he asked me in Spanish, motioning me to a chair.

"Both," I replied, and stared at his hair. There was something miraculous about the way it cocked up on top and slicked flat around the ears.

"Which do you read?"

"Both," I answered again.

"No," he said, drumming a long white hand on the tabletop. Gold fuzz sprouted on his knuckles. He was wearing a ring, ponderous as a prime minister's. "You don't understand me. There must be a difference in the level at which you speak and read your two languages." *Ee-dee-oh-muzz.* His Spanish was broad and drawling, like my mother's. He opened a green folder and looked through it, and then switched his questions to English. "What I'm asking you, missy, is which language are you more proficient in? There are no records or tests here."

"I think I'm about the same in both," I said.

"Sir," he said.

"What?"

"I think I am the same in both, sir."

I repeated the phrase after him. I had never heard anyone in the United States of America talk like that. I wanted to fall on the floor and squeal, his words were striking me as so idiotic. But there was nothing amusing about the man.

"Here," he said. "Read to me from this book." He shoved a brown volume across the table, pinched two fingers, and then plucked a white shirt cuff out of his jacket sleeve.

I turned the book in my hands. *Indians of the Great Plains*, the cover announced. I opened it. "What part would you like me to read?" I asked.

"Any page," he said. "Pick one." He sat back and crossed his hands behind his head.

I flipped through, looking at pictures. Somewhere near the middle there was one labeled *Medicine man with a rattle*, or words to that effect. The witch doctor was peeking out of a tepee, holding an artifact. In the foreground, an Indian brave in a loinflap ran down to a river with his hair spread behind him like wings. The text was interesting enough, something like this: *After the last steaming and sweating ceremony, the Indian plunged into water during the summer, or into a snowbank in winter. Thus purified, he was ready to make an offering to the Great Spirit or seek a sign from the Great Beyond.*

I stared at the words and considered my situation. I could read this aloud and be waved into the English stream. It was clearly as simple as that. Or I could play possum, as Grandpa Doc liked to say. Put one over on the prig.

I snapped the book shut and set it down on the table. "I can't read this," I said, and looked up.

"You're not even going to try?"

I shook my head. "Too hard."

"Well, read this, then," he said, and slid another book at me. It was thin and bright as a candied wafer.

I picked it up, leafed through. Then I smoothed it flat on the table in front of me. "Jane ... puh-plays ... wi-i-ith the ... ball."

"I see," he said, after some pages of this. "I thought as much. That will do." He scribbled a long commentary into my file.

I was put into Señora Arellano's class and, for what seemed a very long time, my parents were none the wiser. I toted my children's illustrated *Historia del Perú*, memorizing the whole litany of Inca rulers until I could recite their Quechua names with all the rattletybang of gunfire.

And Margarita Martínez paid attention to me.

Just as Latin America swung into an anticapitalist, anti-*yanqui* era, George and I entered a new phase of our own: We insisted on playing American games only. We had no idea that the political climate in Peru was as inhospitable to the United States as it was. We didn't realize that Peru had had it with the colossus up north.

Three years before, the Central Intelligence Agency had brought down a leftist government in Guatemala, and Peruvian intellectuals were seething about that. Two years before, Fidel Castro had led a band of revolutionaries into southeastern Cuba to gather popular support for an overthrow of U.S.-backed dictator Fulgencio Batista. America was getting too cocky for its Latin neighbors. Insurrection was in the air. In Mexico City, Che Guevara was whipping up a fervor, planning a guerrilla-led revolution against the capitalists, which he hoped would spread like wildfire from Central America down through the Andes to Argentina.

We knew nothing of this. It was odd, then, that we chose this moment to flex our American muscle, leave the Conquista behind, play cowboy. We had exercised, in our own fashion, considerable calculation in this change: We did it to throw our weight around, show our superiority. We were quite successful in this. We were more American than the Americans: more swaggering, more obstreperous, more cowboy than anyone who dared venture onto our little patch of Avenida Angamos. There is one more thing, so clear in retrospect, so unregistered then: I was playing two worlds off the middle. At the Roosevelt School, I was *muy peruana*, careful not to speak English well, hooting at the lumbering Anglos. But once we hit the street, I was a yee-hawin' rodeo, playing Anglo for all I could get.

"I've chawed Big Red," I'd boast to Albertito Giesecke, the angel-faced boy who dreamed of becoming a priest. "I've chawed it and spit it. Real far. Betcha I could hit cow caca if it were a block away. I gotta cousin who larned me how!"

"Our grandpa's a cowboy," we'd crow at anyone who would listen. A cowboy *abuelo*! A living Doc Holliday! He owns a piece of Norteamerica that stretches out as far as the eye can see. He has cattle. He has horses. Drives a big shiny car. Wears a big broad hat. We're better than you.

MARIE ARANA (Lima, Peru; 1949-) is the author of two highly acclaimed books—the memoir *American Chica: Two Worlds, One Childhood* and the novel *Cellophane.* Book editor of the *Washington Post,* Arana has served on the boards of directors of the National Book Critics Circle and the National Association of Hispanic Journalists.

Guillermo Cabrera Infante in the Wonderland of English

— SUZANNE JILL LEVINE —

The late Guillermo Cabrera Infante was known for artful puns and bilinguistic playfulness. We asked his English translator and good friend for her observations on his relationship to the English language.

GUILLERMO CABRERA INFANTE first learned English at the age of 12 shortly after his family moved from the countryside in Gibara, way out east, to a tenement in Havana. Beginning in 1942, his father, a founder of the Cuban Communist Party, insisted his son take English in night school, where the young Guillermo studied the language for four years. The school was in a predominantly Jewish neighborhood and cost 20 cents a month. Initially resistant, the teen-aged Guillermo soon acquired his English teacher's "zest for language," a biographer has written, and he experimented with it for the rest of his life. The textbook he used back then was called *English in a Nutshell.* The word *nutshell* "seemed intriguing to me," he said years later, "because of its exoticism. From then on, that has been my image of English: intriguing exoticism."

Guillermo Cabrera Infante, lithe liberator of language, was first exposed to American culture through the comics, that is, translations of Dick Tracy and Tarzan. His first literary love was Dragon Lady, a silky Oriental in the *Terry and the Pirates* comic strip. In those days, imported popular culture such as movies and comics, like imported high-culture, came in Spanish.

Guillermo's high culture readings soon included works by Edgar Rice Burroughs and William Faulkner, Ernest Hemingway and James Joyce, Laurence Sterne and the pseudonymous Lewis Carroll. But his initial models of linguistic behavior, aside from his young teacher who played with words in both languages, were the beloved stars and secondary actors he encountered in the movies of Classic Hollywood, from the 1930s to the early '50s. A crucial ingredient in Cabrera Infante's attraction to English was his early and everlasting love of popular culture from the United States, music as well as movies. Indeed, his first writing job as a young man was as film reviewer for the journal *Carteles*. As he was fond of saying, he was "born with a silver screen" in his mouth.

By the time the Cuban Revolution triumphed, Cabrera Infante was a fiction writer and director of the literary supplement of *Lunes*, the new revolutionary newspaper. Two years later, though, in 1961, he would join other intellectuals and artists in a protest against censorship, which led to his dismissal from *Lunes* and eventual self-exile from his native land. In 1964, at age 35, by this time a cultural attaché in Belgium, he broke for good with the five-year-old government and never returned to Cuba. Franco's Spain did not offer him asylum because he was considered a Communist—the ironies of politics and individual destiny. His new home became London.

Already a writer in bloom as well as exile in London, Guillermo found English to be not only a defense but, as he once told me, "a liberating literary medium." For this Havanan, exile was not only geopolitical but also linguistic. In English, freed from the restraints and censorship he had experienced in his mother tongue, he could let loose and play with words as nonsense, unbound from deep or emotional associations, set free from meaning, adrift in the sea of diaspora.

While Hollywood English, the American vernacular—particularly wise-cracking New Yorkese—was Guillermo's favorite English, he came to master and love as well its original version: beautifully baroque British. He considered himself, after decades living in London, "as British as muffins."

When he and I first worked together in 1969–1970 on *Three Trapped Tigers*, American English dominated as the language of the translation. By the time we were translating his third work of fiction, *Infante's Inferno*, in the early 1980s, he often preferred British English for its arch puns and precious alliterations. This Proustian work of almost 800 manuscript pages is filled with baroque whorls of memory and multifarious meanderings. In Infante's universe, where Havana was not only hell but also heaven, the only rule was to obey the erotics of language, in which one noun burgeoned into a cluster of vocables and verbs that would not only conjugate but also copulate with one another.

The late Susan Sontag—a longtime friend of Cabrera Infante's—did not at first see eye to eye with this Cuban punster. Back in the guerrilla days of the Cuban Revolution, she visited the island in solidarity with Fidel and made her way up to the Sierra where they first met—Guillermo a skeptical, essentially apolitical local journalist, she a distinguished international intellectual fired up with the political utopianism of that historical moment. Sontag soon changed her opinion: disillusioned after Fidel's authoritarian rhetoric and draconian actions against free speech, by the early 1970s she would concur with her fellow writer and admire Guillermo's courageous stance against the turn of the Castro regime—courageous because he risked all and became a pariah in the community of his Latin American intellectual peers.

But what she admired even more, as she put it, was his "utterly extraordinary…brilliant prose in more than one language." For many friends and readers, he was more than a bilingual writer. Cabrera Infante, who passed away in February 2005 at the age of 75, was indeed, like his fictional Bustrófedon in *Three Trapped Tigers*, a polyglot genius, as well as a sad tiger trapped in exile.

GUILLERMO CABRERA INFANTE (Gibara, Cuba; 1929–2005) was the author of many novels and essays dealing with Cuban life and politics, focusing much of his literary output on the extremities his homeland's society and culture. His books include *Three Trapped Tigers, Holy Smoke, Infante's Inferno*, and *A View of Dawn in the Tropics*. In 1997 he won the Cervantes Prize, awarded for lifetime achievement in the Spanish language.

Translator and author, Prof. **SUZANNE JILL LEVINE** (New York City, New York; 1948-) teaches at the University of California, Santa Barbara. Her books include *The Subversive Scribe: Translating Latin American Fiction* and the literary biography *Manuel Puig and the Spider Woman: His Life and Fictions*. Levine received a Guggenheim Fellowship and the PEN Award for Career Achievement in Hispanic Studies.

Pura Bicultura

– COCO FUSCO –

Excerpted from *English Is Broken Here*

MY POOR GRANDMOTHER. By the time she arrived in New York from Havana via Madrid, American cartoons and daily trips to Washington Square Park had turned my brother and me into nasty little *yanquis*. We answered back–in English. We turned her Spanish admonitions into puns. We liked to shock adults with bad words. She made sure, however, that we called her *mamá*, instead of disrespectfully reminding her of her age by calling her grandma. But it wasn't long before she began to complain to her daughter. "*No puedo con estos niños*," she would say. "*Están demasiado americanizados.*" (I can't deal with these kids. They're too Americanized.)

What could my mother say? Teachers were warning her that our learning abilities would be impaired by our being subjected to more than one language at home. She and my father were more worried about racial questions than linguistic ones. They were frantically looking for a decent school in New York where we wouldn't be bothered continually for being *mulatos*. They pumped our egos like crazy to give us a defense against the idiocies of a racist world. We became expert mimics, aping the melodiously accented English of our elders, on the one hand, and spoofing the attempts of Americans to pronounce Spanish words on the other. (*I Love Lucy* was of course, our favorite TV program.)

We also became great shape–shifters, turning on Latin politeness to impress our American friends' parents, and then reverting to little *yanqui* brats when we wanted to bewilder the latest nana. One of them, Rufina, fled the house after my parents refused to heed her pleas that we children be exorcised. "*Traen el diablo por dentro*," she cried. (They're possessed by the devil.)

Like most immigrant kids, we slid into the gap between languages and cultures with ease. The world around us was already communicating to us that we were better than our relatives because we had English under our belts. Then there were the other markers that distinguished us. *We* didn't live in a barrio, my mother fiercely reminded us, though she had hidden from the real estate agents so that we could get into the neighborhood. Just in case anyone passing by dared to get any wrong ideas, my mother regularly scrubbed the steps and sidewalk in front of the house. My father unrolled an American flag on the appropriate holidays. We went to church with the Irish on Sundays and prayed in English, and we kids went to a mostly Jewish school during the week. Thanks to my parents, I was fairly oblivious to the implications of the looks and comments that show people's prejudice, and, in any case, we somehow managed to believe that we weren't really in America, or that we got here by mistake. "I did apply for other visas...," my mother would say.

America, we believed, was somewhere else. It was in any direction going away from New York. There wasn't anything good to eat there. My mother had spent two years upstate before I was born and still complained that no one there ate garlic or onions and that the people didn't care about other places. They thought all foreign films were pornographic, the kids were ruder than we were, and they didn't even wash their sneakers. That was the North, but we could also forget about the South. One of the first news stories my mother heard when she arrived in the United States was about Emmett Till. We couldn't even think of traveling to a place where black boys got lynched for whistling at white ladies. If we went there, we'd end up in jail or something, I used to imagine.

Behind the walls of our home, walls that shielded us from that America, we made a world where people and things from all different kinds of places met. To us it seemed that someone was always just arriving from somewhere, which meant we had to celebrate. Maybe it was that immigrants and outsiders share certain experiences that tend to make socializing among themselves easier. Maybe it was that recently arrived relatives and friends would descend on us for weeks at a time, providing us with playmates. Visiting could last a day or several weeks, during which time our friends and cousins became our English pupils while we absorbed their nostalgia for a place we'd never seen. As kids, we might have believed that we were better because of our command of English, but people and things from far away attracted us.

The taste we had for the foreign had been cultivated long before we became immigrants. Cuban exiles in Miami embraced American consumerism in their violent rejection of *el comunismo*, but there was an older tradition, maintained by many, of always looking outward for culture—to France, preferably, but most places on "the Continent" would do. We could go to school in America, if necessary, but to be truly worldly, we had to learn European ways. When, as a young adult, I returned from a semester's study in Paris, my aunt took out her finest china to serve me coffee and sweets. Eight months away and suddenly I was a specially honored guest. My newly acquired French impressed everyone much more than my English ever had. I didn't realize at the time that in their minds I had fulfilled an entirely criollo dream.

COCO FUSCO (Havana, Cuba; 1960-) is an accomplished author and performance artist whose avant-garde and postmodern works have been exhibited for audiences at museums, galleries, and streetfront theaters internationally. Her books include *English Is Broken Here* and *The Bodies That Were Not Ours, and Other Writings*. She was the editor of *Corpus Delecti: Performance Art of the Americas* and now serves as associate professor at Columbia University's School of the Arts.

Aria

— RICHARD RODRIGUEZ —

Excerpted from *Hunger of Memory: The Education of Richard Rodriguez*

I LEARNED MY FIRST WORDS OF ENGLISH over-hearing my parents speak to strangers. At five years of age, I knew just enough English for my mother to trust me on errands to stores one block away. No more.

I was unable to hear my own sounds, but I knew very well that I spoke English poorly. My words could not stretch far enough to form complete thoughts. And the words I did speak I didn't know well enough to make into distinct sounds.

For me there were none of the gradations between public and private society so normal to a maturing child. Outside the house was public society; inside the house was private. Just opening or closing the screen door behind me was an important experience. I'd rarely leave home all alone or without reluctance....Nervously, I'd arrive at the grocery store to hear there the sounds of the gringo—foreign to me—reminding me that in this world so big, I was a foreigner. But then I'd return. Walking back toward our house, climbing the steps from the sidewalk, when the front door was open in summer, I'd hear voices beyond the screen door talking in Spanish. For a second or two, I'd stay, lingering there, listening. Smiling, I'd hear my mother call out, saying in Spanish, "Is that you, Richard?" All the while, her sounds would assure me: You are home now; come closer, inside. With us.

I remember many nights when my father would come back from work, and I'd hear him call out to my mother in Spanish, sounding relieved....Some nights I'd jump up just at hearing his voice. With *mis hermanos* I would come running into the room where he was with my mother. Our laughing (so deep with pleasure!) became screaming. Like others who know the pain of public alienation, we transformed the knowledge of our public separateness and made it consoling—the reminder of intimacy.

Supporters of bilingual education today imply that students like me miss a great deal by not being taught in their family's language. What they seemed not to recognize is that, as a socially disadvantaged child, I considered Spanish to be a private language. What I needed to learn in school was that I had the right—and the obligation—to speak the public language of los gringos....What I did not believe was that I could speak a single public language.

Fortunately, my teachers were unsentimental about their responsibility. What they understood was that I needed to speak a public language. So their voices would search me out, asking me questions. Each time I'd hear them, I'd look up in surprise to see a nun's face frowning at me. I'd mumble, not really meaning to answer. The nun would persist, "Richard, stand up. Don't look at the floor. Speak up. Speak to the entire class, not just to me!" But I couldn't believe that the English language was mine to use. (In part, I did not want to believe it.) I continued to mumble. I resisted the teacher's demands. (Did I somehow suspect that once I learned public language my pleasing family life would be changed?) Silent, waiting for the bell to sound, I remained dazed, diffident, afraid.

Three months. Five. Half a year passed. Unsmiling, ever watchful, my teachers noted my silence. They began to connect my behavior with the difficult progress my older sister and brother were making. One Saturday morning three nuns arrived at the house to talk to our parents. Stiffly, they sat on the blue living room sofa....I overheard one voice gently wondering, "Do your children speak only Spanish at home, Mrs. Rodriguez?" While another voice added, "That Richard especially seems so timid and shy."

That Rich-heard!

With great tact the visitors continued, "Is it possible for you and your husband to encourage your children to practice their English when they are home?" Of course, my parents complied. What would they not do for their children's well-being? And how could they have questioned the Church's authority which those women represented? In an instant they agreed to give up the language (the sounds) that had revealed and accentuated our family's closeness. The moment after the visitors left, the change was observed. "*Ahora,* speak to us *en inglés,*" my father and mother united to tell us.

At first it seemed a kind of game. After dinner each night, the family gathered to practice "our" English. (It was still then *inglés,* a language foreign to us, so we felt drawn as strangers to it.) Laughing, we would try to define words we could not pronounce. We played with strange English sounds, often over-anglicizing our pronunciations. And we filled the smiling gaps of our sentences with familiar Spanish sounds. But that was cheating, somebody shouted. Everyone laughed. In school, meanwhile, like my brother and sister, I was required to attend a daily tutoring session. I needed a full year of special attention. I also needed my teachers to keep my attention from straying in class by calling out, Rich-heard—their English voices slowly prying loose my ties to my other name, its three notes, Ri-car-do. Most of all I needed to hear my mother and father speak to me in a moment of seriousness in broken—suddenly heartbreaking—English. The scene was inevitable: One Saturday morning I entered the kitchen where my parents were talking in Spanish. I did not realize that they were talking in Spanish, however, until, at the moment they saw me, I heard their voices change to speak English. Those gringo sounds they uttered startled me. Pushed me away. In that moment of trivial misunderstanding and profound insight, I felt my throat twisted by unsounded grief. I turned quickly and left the room. But I had no place to escape to with Spanish. (The spell was broken.) My brother and sisters were speaking English in another part of the house.

Again and again in the days following, increasingly angry, I was obliged to hear my mother and father: "*Speak to us en inglés*" (*Speak*). Only then did I determine to learn classroom English. Weeks afterward, it happened: One day in school I raised my hand to volunteer an answer. I spoke out in a loud voice. And I did not think it remarkable when the entire class understood. That day, I moved very far from the disadvantaged child I had been only days earlier. The belief, the calming assurance that I belonged in public, had at last taken hold.

RICHARD RODRIGUEZ (San Francisco, California; 1944-) is the author of *Hunger of Memory, Days of Obligation: An Argument with My Mexican Father,* and *Brown: The Last Discovery of America.* He is an essayist on PBS's nightly *NewsHour,* for which he won a Peabody Award (1997). Rodriguez's many other awards include the Frankel Medal from the National Endowment for the Humanities and a Fulbright Fellowship.

Learning English by the Sinatra Method

— JOSÉ SERRANO —

PEOPLE LEARN SECOND LANGUAGES in strange ways. My experience has to rank among the strangest. I was born and spent my first seven years in Mayagüez, Puerto Rico, where everyone I knew spoke only Spanish.

My father served with the U.S. military in World War II. When he was discharged, he came home with a stack of Frank Sinatra 78-rpm records. Like many Puerto Ricans, music was a huge part of our lives. I spent hours listening to those records and sometimes singing along.

Little did I know, but those records were teaching me the language of the mainland, where my family would soon move. Listening to Sinatra, I learned to pronounce every word distinctly. He never swallowed a syllable. From him I learned rhythms, inflections, and the sounds of a language that was so different from the one I spoke everyday.

Soon we moved to New York, where my education in English continued. I went to a school where everyone spoke English and began to fill out my vocabulary. From Sinatra records I learned to say "Tewsday," like he did, not "Toosday," like everyone else. But even dearer to my heart and similar to my Sinatra English lessons, I listened to Mel Allen do the play-by-play for the Yankees and a young Vin Scully broadcast the Brooklyn Dodgers. Glued to the radio following the exploits of my heroes, I absorbed the language of excitement and disappointment. I learned storytelling and the art of filling dead time.

As I look back on learning a second language, I always think about the doors it opened for me. I can communicate with people from so many different backgrounds and personal experiences in their native tongues. This skill is invaluable as a leader and a community figure. I must listen and talk to people in language they can understand. The words that I choose have more importance to them than when I talk casually with my family or friends. I am making a connection with them through language—and my special awareness of the power and meaning of words serves me in that endeavor.

I have spent considerable energy in Congress beating back efforts to make English the official language of the United States. I always offer an alternative. I want to recognize English as the primary language in the United States and promote the acquisition of English language abilities by all Americans. But perhaps most importantly, my legislative proposal recognizes that multilingualism ensures a greater understanding among the diverse groups of people that compose the fabric of this nation.

Learning and knowing more than one language is an invaluable skill. I often think what my life would have been like if I had never heard Sinatra as a kid. Without those 78s, there's no way of knowing where I would have gone, or what I would have done, but it is safe to say that my life would have been far different.

Frank Sinatra once said, "I think my greatest ambition in life is to pass on to others what I know." I like to live by those words. One of the things that I know is that language is an invaluable tool. The more tools you have for life, the better equipped you are for whatever life will throw at you.

JOSÉ SERRANO (Mayagüez, Puerto Rico; 1943-) grew up in the Bronx. In 1974 he was elected to the New York State Assembly and since 1990 has been a U.S. Congressman. He has sponsored a resolution to encourage the learning of languages beyond English.

From English Gentleman to Zelig

— ALVARO VARGAS LLOSA —

I LEARNED FRENCH BEFORE I LEARNED ENGLISH, and Spanish—my mother tongue—before I learned French, and—to make matters worse—I learned English at the same time that I learned ancient Greek and attempted to learn German. So, if in the course of reading this personal testimony you find something funny with the language, you know where my arcane expressions come from.

My parents, who are great admirers of French culture, sent me to a French school in Lima, Peru, where I received a bilingual education for a few years. At one point I had to take a leave of a few months because my father, a Peruvian-born novelist, accepted an invitation to teach a course at Cambridge University in England. Apparently my brother and I had fun during that short stay in Cambridge, and we expressed an interest in going to boarding school in Britain—at least for a while—sometime in the future. So, a few years later, at the age of 13, I found myself at a British boarding school without speaking a word of English and surrounded by classmates who took me for Pakistani (most of the time) or Italian (occasionally). When I arrived at the school, the first question I was asked—through an interpreter—was if there were any cars in Peru. I responded that we preferred UFOs to avoid rush-hour congestion.

I was terrified in my new school. I vividly remember the first three weeks thinking to myself every night: "Could I actually go dumb and lose the capacity to speak forever if I go for months without being able to speak to anyone?" The thought tormented me for weeks.

a complicated option because mine was an all-male school and hitting the town was impossible—third-form kids were not allowed off the premises except for a quick afternoon stroll. An Italian kid who came to the school with a serious English-language deficit figured out that the only way to beat the obstacles was to declare his love for the French teacher, who was a woman (and perfectly bilingual). Some of my ancient Greek classes were taught by an Englishwoman, so I watched my Italian mate make his move on the French teacher with particular interest, thinking that if it worked for him I might propose to my Greek teacher, too. (The risk, of course, was that she might be inclined to pursue our liaison in ancient Greek!)

The plan was embarrassingly aborted one afternoon when my Italian friend came out of the French class red-faced and with his tail between his legs. "She is married," he said in disgust. "She told me she was flattered but that she is taken. She actually found it rather funny, and I didn't know what to say." Seeing my pal in such a pitiful state, I decided I would not risk rejection, so I scrapped my romantic designs with regard to Miss X (who probably was Mrs. X anyway) and opted for learning English the hard way—that is, wrenching my guts out with books, tapes, video courses, and that irreplaceable method, the humiliation of real-life trial and error.

I did get my English girlfriend the following year. I met her at a party held by the all-girl convent school across the street, to which fourth-form boys from my school were invited. But language played me a bad trick. After not seeing her for a few weeks, I wanted to tell her that I missed her. When I said to her, "I regret you," anglicizing the French word for missing someone, she looked at me in horror and spat out something like: "You are not a gentleman." We never saw each other again.

My passion for languages and my awareness of the disadvantage I was in regarding the rest of the school eventually helped me through. After a brief period during which I took up a Jamaican accent as a way to express admiration for Bob Marley, whom my friends, my brother, and I idolized, I decided to be more British than the Brits. I went on to get an A in my English O-level exams and became quite an expert on John Keats, the Romantic poet, whose "Ode on a Grecian Urn" I would recite to my friends at school all day long ("Though still unravish'd bride of quietness, / Thou foster-child of silence and slow time, / Sylvan historian, who canst thus express / A flowery tale more sweetly than our rhyme").

My accent, of course, was boarding-school British. But this ignominy was quickly corrected a few years later when I spent a semester at Princeton University. There I made friends with a group of left-wing Puerto Ricans who got me active in their various causes (most of which I would frown upon today!). My wife tells me that in matters of language I am a little bit like Zelig, Woody Allen's unforgettable character, and tend to adapt my accent to the surrounding circumstances. In my first visit to my old boarding school in Britain as an alumnus, you can imagine how aghast my teachers were to hear me talk like a Neo-Rican—not to mention the horror of my father, an admirer of all things English.

Since then, my chameleonic English has gone through all sorts of changes of color. At the London School of Economics, where I studied at the end of the 1980s, I fancied a Russian girl—and decided to speak with an impeccable St. Petersburg accent. I later spent time in Florida, where I was the op-ed page editor of a paper known by town folks as "the monster on the bay"—and dutifully spoke with a sort of Andy García accent. Soon after that, I became enamored of Orson Welles's movies and picked up the deep, power-driven Charles Foster Kane accent. Then I went to Spain, where people have many virtues but not the virtue of learning languages, so I added some Castilian ingredients to my already substantial cocktail mix. My years in California probably added a West Coast cachet to that mix, and it is not unlikely that Washington-speak—that horrific cultural disease—has penetrated my English nowadays. It's anybody's guess why I am still able to communicate and my brain has

Although some classmates would talk to me occasionally, the language barrier, and particularly the fact that no one had ever heard of Peru, made me somewhat of a zoological rarity that people tended to stare and make faces at rather than communicate with through the spoken word. I eventually began to do some strange exercises with my mouth to make sure the muscles kept functioning. I practiced in bed and during break time. Finally, I decided there was only one way to make sure I didn't lose the faculty of speech—recording hundreds of tapes with my own voice. I undertook this task with passion for some weeks. After a while, I ran out of things to say to myself, so I started to send my friend Carlos in Lima long letters in the form of recorded cassettes in which I rambled about anything and everything with the sole purpose of protecting my voice. He responded in the same way. Today, I dread the thought of one of those childhood tapes suddenly emerging...and falling into the hands of my enemies.

One day, my French came to the rescue. Since I was by far the best at French because I was the only one who had studied the language for many years, I became useful for a couple of classmates who wanted to impress the teacher. One of them proposed that I teach him French in exchange for helping me learn a bit of English outside the regular school hours. But, of course, this being an English boarding school, there were complex academic requirements that stood in the way of my being able to concentrate on English. I was expected to take up German, ancient Greek, and Latin because the school authorities supposed that a 13-year-old who spoke two languages and was about to learn a third clearly was made for six. As a result there was not much time left for English.

I found myself submerged overnight in Greek betas and thetas, German accusatives and genitives, and Latin cases—while at the same time trying to learn to say "My name is Alvaro Vargas Llosa." Progress was slow, to say the least.

I had been told by authoritative sources that the best way to learn a foreign language was to get a girlfriend who spoke it. That was not yet exploded into a million pieces. "You talk like someone from the International Monetary Fund," one of my wife's friends told me one day. I almost had a heart attack.

Needless to say, I am carefully avoiding putting my children through the same ordeal. So I avoid talking English to them as much as possible with the hope that they can learn to speak like normal people. (I speak to them in Spanish 70 percent of the time and the other 30 percent in English.) Their school, which is multilingual and follows the linguistic immersion program, has kids from all over the world, which makes this an interesting challenge. For the moment, both my kids speak English with a perfect *Simpsons* accent.

I suppose there is one good thing about my chameleonic accent. It reflects my idea of the world. My real wish is that one day all barriers to the free flow of ideas, goods, services, and people will be lifted, and we will all be able to move from one place to the other with total freedom.

ALVARO VARGAS LLOSA (Lima, Peru; 1966-) is senior fellow and director of the Center on Global Prosperity at the Independent Institute in Washington, D.C. He has written for the *Wall Street Journal*, *Granta*, the *International Herald Tribune*, and the *Miami Herald*, where he served on the editorial board. Vargas Llosa's books include *Liberty for Latin America*, *The Madness of Things Peruvian*, *The Myth of Che Guevara*, and, as coauthor, *The Guide to the Perfect Latin American Idiot*.

The Way of the Dinosaurs

— RAFAEL CAMPO —

¡PENDEJO! I SHOUTED THE WORD at the top of my lungs, knowing exactly what kind of reaction it would elicit. *¡Coño!* I added that one for good measure.

My father glowered at me from over his shoulder, taking his eyes off the congested highway just long enough to silence me. We were in the old family Ford LTD, with its textured beige upholstery, rust-red paint job, and brown vinyl hardtop. My younger brothers tried to suppress their giggles, sitting on either side of me in matching pastel-colored polyester miniature leisure suits, their black hair combed back neatly, shiny and hard from a liberal application of my mother's Aquanet hairspray. Around us, the highway stretched toward a horizon crowded with huge scaffolds and water towers and angled cranes, which reminded me of the fossilized dinosaur skeletons I had seen in museums. I was fascinated with dinosaurs, but not for the reasons most six-year-old boys were. To me, they were like my family, which was not yet extinct the way tyrannosaurus and triceratops were, but still on the verge of being lost forever. We were on our way to Elizabeth, New Jersey, to visit my *abuelos*. I was trying my hardest not to have to speak Spanish.

"Don't you talk that way," my father snapped. "We don't use that kind of language in this family!"

I loved being forbidden to speak Spanish. I tried to think of some more choice cusswords, but then thought better of getting my father too angry, noticing the speed with which the trash scattered amidst the tall roadside weeds streaked by. I wanted to speak English, and only English, like all my friends in school did. We lived in a house that my parents had hired some workers to paint a rich shade of gold, with a redwood deck off the back that looked out over a small lake, and neat little black shutters and our own basketball hoop at the end of the sloping driveway. Some of my mother's new friends even drove Cadillacs. Going back to Elizabeth was like going back into prehistory, with its grimy sidewalks, menacing streetwise teenagers, and small, crowded apartments in ugly brick buildings—"tenements," I said quietly to myself, recalling a particularly mellifluent word from the *Merriam-Webster's Dictionary* I was reading cover to cover. I had to admit I liked those words the best.

"What did you say?" My father asked pointedly into the windshield. I was glad he was still angry, and thus still speaking in English. I was grateful not to have to "practice" my Spanish anymore. English, cold, corrective, and formal, was employed whenever anyone in the family got in trouble. With any luck, we would stay in English mode for the rest of the journey.

My family had survived the savage world of Elizabeth, progressing into the secure white suburbs, with its sunny, tree-lined streets. That first winter, I noticed that even the snow stayed whiter longer in our new home; in the city, it was always spoiled within a few hours of falling, streaked with stray dogs' urine and soiled by the soot drifting down from the nearby smokestacks. Even the fire hydrants in Ramsey looked clean, standing at attention like bright red soldiers of the public good. And the trees! Full and healthy—not stunted, or half-dead and ghost-like in places, or missing whole big chunks of branches where errant trucks had plowed past them or black power lines cut through. "Birch," I whispered to myself. "Elm. Linden. Sycamore." I was trying especially hard to memorize the names of trees as I came across them in the dictionary, hoping they would take root in my mind and push out the Spanish. I didn't even know the Spanish names of most of them—*flamboyanes* and palmeros like those my Tía Yoya painted did not grow at all in America, at least in the places we had lived. Spanish, I had decided, was the language of the receding jungle, the language of the distant past, the language of certain extinction.

By learning English, I hoped I would someday forget Spanish completely. In fact, I believed that only by *unlearning* Spanish could I finally leave Cuba behind and become truly American. Though I had never actually been to Cuba, I imagined it was a terribly primitive place. On the maps I had seen, it looked like something unpleasant the United States had inadvertently stepped on. I populated its uncharted mountainous terrain with naked, dark-skinned Indians and all manner of exotic flora and fauna—I even imagined it might be a last refuge for the dinosaurs.

Among the few stories my father told us about Cuba, one of my favorites was about the time he and my abuelo discovered gigantic bones at the far end of their property, where some men had come to dig sand, which my abuelo, ever the entrepreneur, had started to sell. I wasn't sure why anyone would want to buy sand, but that really wasn't the point of the story. I had surprised my father when I used vocabulary words like "entrepreneur"—sometimes I acquired English words he hadn't yet learned himself. Like my abuelo, he was first and foremost a good businessman. Whether those great bones belonged to a dinosaur or not, he couldn't say. In his new life, which involved manufacturing aluminum cans and plastic tubes for soda and toothpaste, there wasn't much time for wondering about dinosaurs—or even for telling us more stories about Cuba.

We were lucky to lose the family ranch in Guantánamo province, I told myself, likewise the small *cabaña* that stood on a nearby cliff overlooking an endless beach, because here in America six-year-old boys were not preyed on by stray velociraptors. It wasn't a good idea to try to get my father to talk about Cuba anyway, because he would usually lapse into Spanish; my mother, who was Italian-American, her skin white enough that in summertime she would freckle instead of tan, would then frown a little if we were all at the dinner table. She had met my father taking a Spanish literature course in college. She was beautiful and very popular, so when my father first called her to ask her out on a date, she didn't really remember who he was. Lots of young men called her asking for dates. I imagined him talking to her on the telephone with his thick accent, trying to persuade her to go to a movie. It's true my father was very handsome, but on the telephone, since she couldn't see his face, all she had was this heavy accent to go by. She almost said no. Therefore, because of Spanish, I might not ever have come into existence.

In my evolutionary view of the world, English had to overcome Spanish in my consciousness. Even though I didn't like girls, I was sure I would need English to survive in other ways. I thought of my abuelo, who was forced to work in a factory that made cheap preformed yellow plastic tables because he couldn't speak English. My abuela didn't have a job at all—not like my mother, who was a substitute teacher at my new school in Ramsey, New Jersey—so she stayed in their apartment all day long, crying a lot over all that they had been forced to leave behind in Cuba. That's why they were poor and had to stay in Elizabeth.

It was my mother who cared most about our intellectual and social advancement in the world. When she packed us into the car, instead of heading south on these same highways, it was northeast to New York City and its magical sites and endless museums. Besides being a teacher, she was an artist. Dominating our living room was her dramatic painting of a bullfight, with its blood-red background and glittering golds and silvers in the matador's costume. She took us to the Metropolitan Museum of Art, where I copied her pensive staring at the large canvases depicting places all over the world except, it seemed, Cuba. Even the dry, dusty expanses of Spain appeared; the Spaniards themselves, however, as painted by El Greco and Goya, and even Velázquez, seemed malformed, brutish, and backward.

Even better than the art museums was the Museum of Natural History. I savored one particular memory of my first visit there. I'd run shouting into the cavernous room where the massive dinosaur fossils were exhibited, calling out the name of each specimen and describing its habitat, range, and feeding preferences (*Carnivorous! Herbivorous! Omnivorous!*). The polished floors and the towering columns only emphasized the distance we had traveled, and from cold-blooded reptiles with brains the size of a pea to human beings with the capacity for self-awareness, from the overgrown jungles of Cuba to the epitome of culture and learning that was New York. I remembered the proud look on my mother's face as one of the museum's staff—surely an expert on dinosaurs himself—commended me for my clear pronunciation of so many difficult names and my mastery of scientific terminology. We all celebrated afterwards with ice cream sundaes, a delicacy far more decadent than the shaved ice in a paper cone doused in fruit syrup that was my father's treat years ago on visits to Havana with his family.

Soon I recognized the huge green sign for Elizabeth (and not the George Washington Bridge) as it flashed above us, and then heard the tinny clinking of the LTD's blinker as my father signaled to exit the highway. I tried to resist the surprising slight anticipation I began to feel as we neared the Cuban neighborhood. My father called back to us to lock the car doors as more and more buildings, old decrepit warehouses and boarded-up strip malls, began to enclose us. We were almost there.

My abuela had probably prepared the usual elaborate feast of *pernil, congrí, maduros*, and *yuca con mojo*. It always amazed me how she could produce such a sumptuous meal from the tiny kitchen at the back of their apartment. They would be playing old Cuban LPs, and in the middle of dinner, my abuelo would stand and then sweep her up into his arms, and they would dance for a few moments alongside the table that stretched into the living room, as they didn't have a big dining room with a proper dining room table like ours.

There would be Spanish newspapers lying about, drooping over the edges of those small plastic yellow tables brought home from the factory. My abuelo was always reading, though I still disbelieved my father's boast that he had a fancy library filled with books in their old ranch house in Cuba. Then, my abuela would cry a little, smiling through her tears at all of us kids as she settled back down in her chair.

Later, my abuelo would want to walk down the block to the Cuban bakery with us. The street they lived on was still relatively safe, and we would pass beneath windows with blinking colored Christmas lights framing them from the inside, even when it wasn't wintertime. Behind the tall glass of the bakery's display cases, countless varieties of *pastelitos* were arranged, gleaming like the fancy porcelain figurines my mother collected, each variety a different geometric shape: *carne, jamón y queso, chorizo, pollo*, and my Tía Marta's favorite, guava. Though we couldn't eat another bite, my brothers and I would still clamor to pick out our favorites, which were then neatly boxed and tied up with a red-and-white string for us to take home. While we would be making our choices, jostling each other for the best position in front of the glass, my grandfather would argue in Spanish about politics with the owner of the bakery, drinking coffee out of a tiny Dixie cup and smoking a cigarette. On the way back I clutched his hand, which felt as hard and strange-shaped as one of my toy dinosaurs.

Of course, the hardest part of these visits was when my abuelos would speak to me in Spanish, and I would have to pretend I didn't understand them. If truly mastering English meant truly unlearning Spanish, then I could make no exceptions. I knew this meant I would get to hear even fewer stories about Cuba, but even then I understood we were never going back there. My abuela would try for a while, telling me how much she loved me, asking me about what I was learning in school, but I would go on helping her wash the dishes with a perplexed look on my face. Sometimes I would just ignore her, drawing and coloring dinosaurs fierce reds and yellows and greens in a small corner of the kitchen table she'd clear off for me. Or I would interrupt her to inquire, standing on my tiptoes and looking out the window over the sink, "Isn't that a maple tree, Grandma?" knowing perfectly well she couldn't understand me.

I liked being in the kitchen with her, enveloped in the strong fragrances of garlic and cumin and olive oil, and the sing-song lilt of her voice, but I reminded myself that I was helping her really because it was the least I could do, especially if I wasn't going to speak Spanish with her. Plus she had already suffered so much. Spanish was the language of her suffering, it was the language of betrayal. Spanish was the history that didn't really exist, vanished forever like "the missing link," or like other fossils of whole species of dinosaurs that the world would never know. It was best to unlearn this primal tongue, the deliberate loss of which became the genesis of how I learned English.

Now, almost 40 years later, when I try to remember an intentionally forgotten Spanish word, what I first recall is the heartbroken expression on my abuela's kind face.

Essayist and poet **RAFAEL CAMPO** (Dover, New Jersey; 1964-) teaches and practices general internal medicine at Harvard Medical School and Beth Israel Deaconess Medical Center in Boston. He is the author of *Diva, The Enemy,* and other books of poetry, as well as *The Desire to Heal,* a collection of essays. He is the winner of two Lambda Literary Awards, a Guggenheim Fellowship, and the Annual Achievement Award from the National Hispanic Academy of Arts and Sciences.

My Two Tongues /
Mis dos lenguas:
On How I Came to
Have a Forked Tongue

— LILIANA VALENZUELA —

I WAS A MIDDLE-CLASS CHILD, growing up in the sixties, aware of other languages from an early age. In most Mexican private schools, English is mandatory and often the most important criterion by which parents choose a school. Public schools also teach English, but the instruction is not as demanding as it is in most private schools. I attended private schools. Most middle-class families in Mexico send their children to private school, and we were no exception, even though that meant my father held two jobs his entire life. Although my mother was a chemist by university training and a would-be singer in her heart of hearts, she was happy to stay home and raise a family.

My sisters and I attended a private all-girl Catholic elementary school run by nuns, and my brother, a private all-boy school. Later we all transferred to a coed, lay private middle school and high school run by Spanish refugees who had fled the Franco dictatorship. My mother was a devout Catholic, my father a lapsed Protestant, and many of my new classmates in this school were Jewish, so I was also exposed to other religions and ways of thinking—not always the case in predominantly Catholic Mexico. The school had some excellent English teachers, and its atmosphere of profound humanism, idealism, and tolerance made a deep impression on me.

I remember my stout kindergarten English teacher singing "My Bonnie Lies over the Ocean" accompanying herself on her accordion. She also sang:

Pollito chicken, *gallina* hen
lápiz pencil, and *pluma* pen.

I have fond memories of playing "*turista*" with my best friend, bedecking ourselves in plastic multicolored necklaces—the more the better—sunglasses and lipstick and walking around pretending to speak English, full of soft r's, soft shhh sounds, and lots of mock "w" sounds too: arrshshshshwarsh, wooollorrrrash…. Aside from the tourists on whom we would eavesdrop at the Zócalo or in the floating gardens of Xochimilco, several of my mother's sisters had married americanos and had moved to the other side. They would come to visit from time to time, and we were able to confirm that the English we were taught at the nuns' elementary school would not take us very far in life. Nonetheless, our *tías'* visits planted in us a *semillita*, a seedling, of curiosity and a love of language.

My father was trilingual. As a young immigrant from the Gulf State of Tabasco pursuing a college education in the bustling capital in the 1950s, my father studied English at the Instituto Mexicano-Norteamericano de Relaciones Culturales and French at the Instituto Francés de la América Latina (IFAL). His French and his engineering degree landed him a fellowship in petroleum studies in Paris. When he returned, he married my mother, who was from Guanajuato and who had studied French at the IFAL with him. I remember growing up with books in Spanish, an English encyclopedia that I could never totally understand, and a few books in French around the house. One was called *Paris des Reves*. I always thought the title meant "París al revés" or "Paris backwards," instead of "Paris of dreams." My parents would sometimes sing in English and French, as well as Spanish, of course, songs such as "Chattanooga Choo Choo" in two-voice harmony, and "Chevalier de la Table Ronde." The language spoken at home, however, was always Spanish.

Multilingual people we happened to know were looked up to as intelligent and worldly, qualities to aspire to. Language study was encouraged in our home. On Sundays, my father would show us movies of his wanderings through Europe in his quaint little Citröen "Deux Cheveaux" car, way back when he was a graduate student, narrated with *lujo de detalles* and a changing set of characters. This experience whetted our appetite for foreign travel and languages all the more. One of my uncles was said to know German and to have worked for a German firm. I enjoyed asking him to teach me words in German, French, and English. I don't know if he actually spoke any of these fluently, but he knew enough to keep an eight-year-old entertained, counting to 20 and practicing greetings.

In both Mexico and the United States, children learn the value of one language over another early on. As a young child in Mexico, I was aware of the prominence that English held in our lives as the door to "progress": education, jobs, travel, opportunities, college, popular books, textbooks, and the world at large. By contrast, many bilingual children in the United States often perceive Spanish as having secondary status in society and choose to speak English exclusively, even when addressed in Spanish. They are acutely aware that even in our politically correct society, where the tide has shifted and Spanish is viewed more favorably than ever before, speaking Spanish brands them as second-class citizens, despite all our efforts to convince them to the contrary.

I spoke Spanish exclusively with my own two children until they were four years old. After they started school and became immersed in English, it became harder and harder for them to reply to me in Spanish. As their vocabulary in English grew exponentially, their Spanish vocabulary shrank and they were unable to express more complex ideas or concepts with their limited Spanish. They both still speak Spanish when we go on extended vacations to visit family in Mexico, but I'm painfully aware that we are swimming against the current, as it were, struggling to preserve the language and culture for this next generation. Although my 12-year-old son goes to a highly integrated school where diversity is the norm, the more I try to get him to speak Spanish, the more he resists. The more I try to teach him about Mexico and our customs, the more he pushes back. Deep down I know my children have received a good foundation, but how much is enough?

Growing up in Mexico, it would never have occurred to me to feel ashamed of speaking Spanish. The language was my world and I lived in it effortlessly: lulled by my mother's lullabies, her radio programs keeping her company while doing her chores, the rambunctious sounds of my brother and sisters, the stern nuns' voices at school, the words to the Mexican national anthem, and the vendors selling their wares: *elooootes, se afilan cuchiiiillos...camooootes, peines a dos por uno.* Spanish was like the smell of cilantro flavoring the rice cooking in the kitchen, permeating every corner of our home.

Back when I was in high school, the curriculum forced us to trudge through the medieval poem "Cantar de mio Cid" and literature from the Spanish Golden Age before we could enjoy the discovery of contemporary Latin American fiction writers like Rosario Castellanos, Carlos Fuentes, and Julio Cortázar. We also discovered favorite poets such as Mario Benedetti, Federico García Lorca, and Pablo Neruda. For my English teacher, I had the fortune to have a former Harlem Globetrotter basketball star who somehow ended up in Mexico teaching English and coaching basketball at our school. He was also the only black American I knew growing up. His full name, as he jokingly recited it, was "David Winburn Junior Master Taylor Patrick Leave," a tongue-twister my youngest sister loved to chant over and over, but to us he was simply el teacher. With a smooth American accent and a velvety voice, and huge elongated fingers he would gesture with like a fan, he introduced us to writers such as James Baldwin, John Steinbeck, Ernest Hemingway, and Daphne du Maurier. There was something in the apparent simplicity and directness of the language that captivated me. I felt like I could relate to these characters even though they were situated in such foreign places. El teacher nurtured the love of literature without burdening us with unnecessary memorization of authors, eras, and major works, which were imposed on us in Spanish literature. Here, it was simply, *literature*. And we got to react to it in a more direct way. I'm not sure my classmates shared this passion, but another literary seed was planted in me.

I started writing poetry and short stories when I was about 24, although I had kept a journal for most of my life. Almost simultaneously, I started to translate them into English, mostly for the benefit of workshops or writing-group members. Translating ended up being my *oficio* and calling as a *mujer de letras*, together with writing fiction, poetry, essays, and reviews. In short, I became a language fanatic—a writer with too many words in both languages in my head, all trying to come out at the same time. I am now so in love with language that poetry is to me a playful dance with words and languages, a constant milking of both languages, juxtaposing them, going back and forth between ideas, images, horrified and fascinated by the brilliance of words, their gut-wrenching power, their shimmering beauty.

English is the language I've set parallel roots in, by choice and circumstance. At one point I felt I was in danger of losing my writing voice altogether in either Spanish or English. I froze for a few years; I agonized over which language to write in, and in which genre. New experiences in my adopted country demanded to be put down in English, sometimes with a smattering of Spanish. Yet my dreams and poems are often still in Spanish.

Eventually I came to trust whichever language my initial impulse led me into. Some stories have come out in English, some poems in

Spanish, some flow from one to the other in an organic way, others seem destined to be in one language only. I try not to block the process once it's happening. As in the famous ad, I *just do it*. I believe it is possible today to have a chance as a bilingual poet in the United States, as well as dual writing careers in English and Spanish. A rather ambitious goal perhaps, but sometimes I feel like I have no choice but to do just that. After all, Kafka, Conrad, and Nabokov all chose to write and create their art in their adopted languages, and what a magnificent job they did. *Poco a poco*, I tell myself. One heart, one mind, two tongues. Or, perhaps, like a snake, I'm an animal with a forked tongue, tasting and sensing, responding to the dual stimuli of a borderland existence.

LILIANA VALENZUELA (Mexico City, Mexico; 1960-) has tranlated into Spanish contemporary works by Sandra Cisneros (*Caramelo*), Denise Chávez (*The Last of the Menu Girls*), Yxta Maya Murray (*The Conquest*), and a basketful of young adult fiction by Julia Alvarez. She lives in Austin, where she graduated from the University of Texas with a bachelor's and master's degrees in cultural anthropology and folklore.

Don Francisco's Six Steps to Better English

— MARIO KREUTZBERGER ("DON FRANCISCO") —

IN TODAY'S WORLD to be bilingual is an advantage, especially if our second language is English. Looking back, I remember that in public schools in my native Chile, we were offered both English and French. But we practiced language only in the classroom.

Years later, experience taught me that formal knowledge, although it gave me a firm foundation, was very far from being a second language. When I was 19, my father sent me to New York to take a technical administration class in men's fashions. Before the trip I decided to improve my English with a conversation course at the Chilean-North American Institute in Santiago.

It was enough for me just to arrive in New York and take a taxi to understand that what I knew would scarcely serve me to ask for the check in a restaurant or where the bathroom was. All of a sudden I realized that I knew very little English.

I had to take emergency measures—my classes were starting in one week and I simply couldn't fail. The need compelled me to create a unique system that helped enormously. Perhaps it can be helpful to others who are in a similar situation.

Looking back, I can safely say that I had six resources that helped me in important ways:

1. Buying a pocket dictionary and a standard encyclopedia for my hotel room.

2. Talking with Anglos who didn't speak Spanish.
3. Watching and listening to English-language television and radio every day.
4. Reading newspapers and magazines and trying to translate everything that was going on.
5. Keeping a dictionary with the words that I learned every day. I took notes in a small pocket notebook during the day, then copied everything at night into a regular notebook that I alphabetized.
6. Translating everything that I saw: signs in shop windows, neon signs, ads in the subway, everything. (Remember, this was 1959, and electronic agendas, computers, BlackBerrys, and all that didn't exist.)

My system was simple. On my way down to the subway, I would look for older people who didn't seem in a hurry and I would ask them how to get to an address. They tried to explain, and almost always they would ask me who I was, where was I from, and what was I doing in New York. Each time I understood a little more and I could answer a little better.

At the end of each day, I'd incorporated new words into my dictionary and prepare the sentences that would start a new conversation the next day, again supposedly asking for directions. I complemented this routine by watching television to train my ear to the English accent of the North American.

Every night I chose ten new words that I had incorporated in my dictionary, and I'd try to use them in my increasingly lengthy subway dialogue. Also, talking with people at my hotel improved my pronunciation and added phonics to the dictionary.

The system really worked for me. After 90 days I could navigate pretty well, and after a year I felt I had enough ability to join in conversations and understand almost everything being said.

At the end of 1961 I had the opportunity to start in television as a host back home in Chile. I held that position for 24 years. During that time I lost some of my English for lack of practice, though I did use it during trips, especially when I had to translate the interviews I did for the "La Cámera Viajera" segment. In 1986 an opportunity opened up for me to work for Spanish-language television in Miami. As a result, I renewed my interest in improving myself in the language of Shakespeare. I took courses in grammar and conversation and continued with my system of new words that I'd add to my dictionary.

I have arrived at this conclusion: there isn't a subject or theme that one finishes learning; it has to be continuously worked on day in and day out.

I should add: The past we knew, the present we are living, but the future gives us the opportunity to live another day and to learn something that we didn't already know, whether it's English, Spanish, or anything else.

MARIO KREUTZBERGER (Talca, Chile; 1940-), known to television viewers as DON FRANCISCO, hosts the enormously popular weekly three-hour Miami-based audience participation variety show *Sabado Gigante*. He was elected national vice president of the Muscular Dystrophy Association (2000) and named a Champion of Health of the Americas by the Pan-American Health Organization.

What Happened to Our Old Life?

— GIGI ANDERS —

Excerpted from *Jubana!: The Awkwardly True and Dazzling Adventures of a Jewish Cubana Goddess*

I HAD A CUBAN REFUGEE child's work to do: Learning *inglés*. Someone had taken pity on my financially ruined family and blessed us with a small black-and-white Motorola TV. I religiously watched *Captain Kangaroo* and *The Lucy Show*, with Mr. Green Jeans and Mr. Mooney. I listened to Ella Fitzgerald records—my fave was "A Tisket, a Tasket." And there was an older girl who lived in our ugly brick building on Southeast Mississippi Avenue, Pamela, whom I met one day on the elevator. She marveled at my pearl earrings, remarking that she'd never seen such a tiny girl with pierced ears before. At the playground behind the dump that was our first real residence in the United States, all the other kids were equally mesmerized, taking turns touching my earlobes just to see if my pierced ears were real. I thought they were weird for not having pierced ears. Didn't all normal girls have them? These children are so childish and unsophisticated, I thought. They really need to get out more.

Papi and Mami always left and entered the building by way of the basement laundry room. They didn't want to socialize with the truckers, soldiers, and electricians—i.e., our neighbors—who assembled daily on aluminum folding chairs out front, drinking beer. It was hardly a matter of snobbery on my parents' part; what the hell did they have in common with rednecks, or them with us? Plus, who knew, there might be another coup in Cuba and soon we could put this fucking nightmare behind us and return to our normal lives.

Meanwhile, until we bought our new coats, Mami was still using Baba Dora's mink stole to ward off the cold, and Mami's diamond engagement ring, which she'd managed to smuggle out of Cuba, was the size of a Ping-Pong ball. It was all just too much to explain to outsiders. The americanos—especially these charming neighbors of ours—would never understand it.

Some years ago, Mami, a civil servant, finally caved to the constant comment of people about her ring and placed it in a safe-deposit box in the bank. Her replacement diamond ring is actually bigger than the original and so sparkly it could blind you. She keeps it that way with Windex. That is because it is a fabu-fake from Bijoux Terner, the *only* costume jewelry boutique that any self-respecting Miami *cubanita-cubanasa* would *ever* set a spike heel in. The Terners are old friends of my mom's, and they, too, arrived in this country with nada. Theirs is a really good story, how they saw gold in them thar fakes and built up this ersatz jewelry empire. The boutiques—there are several scattered across Miami—are the size of warehouses. You go crazy in there because there's just so much great stuff—Chanel knockoffs, amazing hair ornaments, all the grooviest, trendiest accessories you see in fashion mags—and the prices are so cheap.

But in those early days in Southeast, what little we owned and wore was real. Poor = real; settled = fake. Very strange. So that when my new friend Pamela complimented my pearl earrings or my 18-karat yellow and rose-gold ID bracelets (which all Cuban babies wear) as we dangled from the jungle gym outside or played inside with her many dolls—so many dolls! I was in heaven!—it was real. Pamela was the daughter of a sergeant stationed at Bolling Air Force Base in nearby Southwest Washington, DC. She was nice and pretty and blonde. She gave me a bunch of books I still own: *Pat the Bunny, Andersen's Fairy Tales, Tales from Grimm, The Cat in the Hat, Curious George, Ellen's Lion, Just So Stories*, and *Charlotte's Web*....

Pamela helped me make the transition into my second language by reading English-language stories to me and making me read others back to her, correcting me whenever I made a mistake. The most useful and helpful book she gave me was *The Cat in the Hat Beginner Book Dictionary*; the basic words—*camp, friend, happy*—were each illustrated and used in sentences. I loved that book. Or rather, I relied on it to expand my new lexicon. To master English was the most important and intense thing for me then. Learning it, getting it, using it confidently was as exciting and unfolding an experience as I could imagine, like Helen Keller making the connection between water and the word *water*. I deeply identified with Helen Keller, as I did with Carson McCullers's Frankie, and those two characters would become more significant in my life as time went on.

Emily Dickinson, with whom I share a birthday, wrote, "There is no Frigate like a Book / To take us Lands away," and truly, little made me happier than getting into bed with a pile of books. Whenever Mami went someplace she'd ask, "What do joo want me to breengh joo back?" and I'd always answer, "A new book." Unknown to any of us, at least consciously, I was already moving in a certain direction; my vocation was calling me by my name. When your child would rather stay inside reading books than go out and play kickball with the neighborhood kids—it's a sign. Mami would say, "Joo have to get out DER!" and I'd say, "Out *where?*"

…It's hard to go from that height down to kids with unpierced earlobes fighting over who's safe and who's out on the street. Who cared?

Unlike me, my parents would always have problems moving between Spanish and English. As recently as two years ago, when a raccoon found its way into their suburban house, my broom-wielding father chased it through the living room yelling "¡*Vamos*! ¡*Vamos*!" while my mother shouted, "Speak to eet een Eengleesh!"

What happened to our old life? The balmy days of ease and Mami pushing me in a stroller on Saturday mornings with the tropical sun freckling our skin as we squint along the beach. Stopping at a café and kissing and hugging your girlfriends, Estela, Berta, the drop-dead beauties Anitica and Nedda, all with their babies, the sun sparkling off the women's blood red fingernails and smiling red lips. Somewhere, the handsome, strapping men were off playing clickety-clack dominós, puffing masculine clouds of earthy tobacco, punching the air with the pungent bouquet of cigar smoke. I sucked on the nipple of my guava nectar *con vitaminas* and drifted off to the song of surf, golden bracelets, and women's laughter; the perfume of Agua de Violetas, espresso, L'air du Temps, and imported cigarettes.

GIGI ANDERS (Havana, Cuba; 1957-) is the author, most recently, of *Men May Come and Men May Go...But I've Still Got My Little Pink Raincoat: Life and Love In and Out of My Wardrobe*. Her previous title was *Jubana! The Awkwardly True and Dazzling Adventures of a Jewish Cubana Goddess*, released in paperback as *Be Pretty, Get Married, and Always Drink TaB: A Memoir*. She has written extensively for magazines as well as newspapers in Washington, D.C., and Raleigh, North Carolina.

Baseball Taught Me English

— ORLANDO CEPEDA —

I PLAYED MY FIRST year of professional baseball in 1955. This was in Kokomo, Indiana, Class D ball. That was also the very same year I moved to this country. I did not speak any English at the time. I later learned English because I was not afraid to talk to anyone.

I experienced many different trials when I first came to this country due to the fact that I did not speak English, and also because of my skin color. At that time I was the only Latino on my baseball team. I was not allowed to stay in the same hotels as my teammates due to me being Latino and black. My first words in English were, "I'm hungry." In restaurants the only two things I knew how to order were chile con carne and apple pie a la mode. I ate that for two months straight. Then, in the same town, I found a Chinese restaurant and switched to eating rice everyday.

I did not have a television back home in Puerto Rico, so the first program I saw in this country was *The Eddie Fisher Show*. I learned a few English words thanks to that program—phrases like "Thank you very much" and "Good night." Going to the movie theaters was not an option for me at the time, because the three times that I tried to go they would not let me in due to my skin color. Another event that I went through early on was getting lost on a Greyhound bus traveling from Florida to Salem, Virginia. I was lost for three days with no clothing except what I wore on my back. The English sounded totally new to me. American radio was a way for me to learn new words.

Back when I was 14 years old, I was very frustrated because I had a lot of knee problems, and I wanted to be a professional baseball player just like my father, the great Pedro "Perucho" Cepeda. My idols were and still are my mother and father. Especially my mother. She taught me how to love. She taught me religion, and how to help others.

I have read many great books in my lifetime, but my favorite of all time is called *The Buddha in Your Mirror*. When I am feeling low, I reread that book and it makes me feel great!

The reason I speak English today is that I was born with the talent to play baseball and was able to come to this country and make a living doing what I love. When you speak English, you can travel anywhere in the world and people will know what you are talking about.

The San Francisco Giants organization helped me formally and taught me the American way. I was very lucky and fortunate to have some great teammates in all my years of playing baseball on various teams. I am happy to say that to this day I am still great friends with most of them! Max Lopez, who used to work with the Giants, came to spring training every year and gave us English classes.

I still reside in the San Francisco Bay Area, giving back to the town that gave so much to me. Every day that goes by, I give thanks in my prayers to my mother and father, without whom I would not be the man that I am today. English is my second language, so naturally I am still more comfortable speaking Spanish. At baseball clinics, and when visiting schools and hospitals, I now speak in both Spanish and English to encourage the youth.

ORLANDO CEPEDA (Ponce, Puerto Rico; 1937-) played major league baseball for 16 years beginning in 1958 with the San Francisco Giants and six other teams. He was National League Most Valuable Player (1967) and a Hall of Fame inductee in 1999, and he is the author of three memoirs including *High and Inside: Orlando Cepeda's Story*.

Ghost Boy

— FRANCISCO GOLDMAN —

MY AUNT LEE AND UNCLE JOHN, a surgeon, were the high culture branch of the family. She was a violinist, he a cellist, and they met playing in a Depression-era chamber orchestra in Boston. Aunt Lee, my father's oldest sister, was from a Russian Jewish immigrant family that fled the czarist pogroms, and Uncle John was a Russian Catholic émigré who'd left after the Bolshevik Revolution. They lived in a colonial house in Concord, Massachussetts, that bore a historical plaque dating it to the 1700s. I used to imagine that it had once been the home of a minuteman citizen-soldier of the American Revolution, the true ones who fired the shot heard round the world.

In my first memories of Uncle John, from when I was four or five, he was already old, with snowy hair, a walrus mustache, round reddish cheeks, and jolly blue eyes. Uncle John was ten years older than Aunt Lee, who was older than my father, and my father was born in 1910. So Uncle John was old enough to remember a 19th-century boyhood. I recall a framed photograph of him in a military officer's dress uniform. For a long time I thought this was a picture of Uncle John in the czar's navy, but that is probably wrong. I vaguely recall someone once telling me that that picture was from World War II, when Uncle John served as a U.S. military surgeon.

I loved visiting that old house, with its low ceilings, thick wood beams, and big brick fireplace, the rooms filled with musical instruments, books, old European tchotchkes, and a mounted 19th-century navigator's globe that was almost as tall as myself. It was like a house in an old fairy tale, where maybe the musical instruments came alive at night. Portly Uncle John dozed off in his armchair.

Then my little sister, Barbara, and I would draw close to listen to him chortling and muttering to himself in Russian. What was he dreaming of? Here's a clue: One time he switched to English, and we heard him cooing, "Oh Tootsie, oh Tootsie."

Uncle John and Aunt Lee never had children. When I was 12, they gave me *The Hobbit* as a birthday present, which became my favorite book. (My parents wouldn't have known about Tolkien.) I was about 15 when Uncle John died. My sister, serious about music, was always especially close to Aunt Lee, who gave her violin lessons and a violin. When I was in college, Aunt Lee passed away. My sister inherited a number of her belongings: classical and opera records, books, paintings. (I took for myself a hardcover edition of *War and Peace* in Constance Garnett's translation.) My sister also inherited an old reel-to-reel tape recorder and boxed recordings of musical performances, some of Uncle John and Aunt Lee playing duets. There were also family recordings: another uncle telling war stories, or describing a recent family trip. There was at least one tape-recording of my family, from when my sister, mother, and I had finally returned to Boston from Guatemala to live after a long separation from our father. I was about four. In that recording, I was much taken with some recent trip to a zoo, which I went on about at length, in effortless Spanish—until my mother's voice interrupted, prodding me to speak in English.

"And we went to *de zooooo*," I obliged, in an astonishingly strong Guatemalan accent, "and we saw *de mohnnn-keeeeeees*."

It was strange to be a college student, listening to your four-year-old self do something that you couldn't do anymore: speak fluent Spanish. It made sense that I'd learned Spanish before English, because by the time I was four most of my life had been spent in Guatemala. But it wasn't until I heard that tape that I really knew that about myself. Where had that little boy's Spanish gone? Where had that boy gone? He was me, but he was also somebody else: somebody who spoke Spanish. Maybe he was still living a parallel life in Guatemala, unaware of his English-speaking double.

My father was 20 years older than my mother. And my mother, like Uncle John, was a Catholic. I spent the first years of my life shuttled between Guatemala City and Massachusetts. Early marital strife between my parents caused these separations. By the time I was three, it seemed decided that my mother, sister, and I were going to be staying in Guatemala permanently. But when I was four I contracted tuberculosis, and that precipitated a move back to Boston and an uneasy parental rapprochement. The shock of dislocation imprinted itself inside me in such a way that I have, I think, an unusual number of vivid memories even from when I was two or so, of my *abuelos'* house in Guatemala City, of airplane flights on Pan Am airliners, of a midwinter move back to an austere little house that I'd never seen before in the Boston suburbs.

As long as I've been conscious of such things, I've had the sense of a double or divided life. Guatemala City and Massachusetts. Catholic and Jewish. Guatemalan and American. Contrasting memories of the populous, pungent patio of my grandparents' house in Guatemala City—chickens, parrots, my pet rabbit, the Indian girls who took care of and fussed over me—and of sitting for hours at the living room window in the Boston suburbs staring out at snow and remote-looking houses that were like mirror images of ours. These are the bedrock images of an inner landscape that I still inhabit as if they are aspects of one singular place. But how true is that if you can speak the language of only one of those places, and not of the other?

The little boy who at some point must have been able to speak both had been cleaved in two: one who spoke English, and the other—vanished! A permanent absence. I was his ghost, and he was mine. In a sense, I've spent the last three decades, during which I've lived as much in Latin America as in the United States, as if on a mission to bring those two boys together again.

Latin Americans are often bewildered by, and a little contemptuous of, all those U.S. Latinos who don't speak Spanish. When you are a "U.S. Latino" who makes his or her living as a writer, it can be pretty embarrassing, if not mysterious.

In my case, it's not a total mystery. In the first grade, I sometimes got Spanish and English words mixed up. And I was being educated in a very white Massachusetts suburban school system. My first-grade teacher was actually very nice, and I will never forget those glorious few weeks when she read us *Charlotte's Web*, a chapter a day, and how smitten I was, pretty Miss Hogarth! But my mother was called into the school by administrators, and told that for my and my sister's benefit, only English should be spoken at home. My mom could speak English, couldn't she? Of course she could—she'd even gone to college in the States. So why were we using Spanish at home? Then, once or twice a week, I was called out of class for sessions with the speech therapist charged with ridding me of my Spanish-speaker's accent. It wasn't as if, at the age of six, there was time for me to learn how to distinguish between English and Spanish words on my own, and how to pronounce them like my classmates. No, this was urgent business.

Speech therapist: *"Say Mother."*
Me: *"Mud-hair."*
Speech therapist: *"Noooo! Mother!"* Smack!
Me: *"Ouch! ¡Vil bruja!"* (Okay, I exaggerate.)

I imagine that all across the USA other kids must have been going through a similar process. What kind of country produces educators who think it necessary to exorcize foreign languages and accents from little children? But, after all, this took place almost half a century ago, when I was in the first grade. Obviously, our country has changed a great deal since then. Americans no longer grow nervous when they hear foreign languages spoken in their streets and schools. It's not like they would ever do anything so silly and superfluous as to encourage Congress and state legislatures to pass laws declaring English our only and official language, for example. It's not as if they would ever criminalize, or stigmatize, people for being native Spanish, French, or Arabic speakers.

A few years ago, a New York City publishing house decided to bring out an English-language translation of a novel by a friend, the exceptional novelist José Manuel Prieto, who grew up in Cuba; was educated in the Soviet Union; became a citizen of Mexico, where he published his first books; and currently lives in New York. (His 12-year-old daughter already speaks four languages!) The publisher chose a supposedly reputable translator, but when José received the first draft of the translation, he was appalled. It was a mess. At one point in his novel, José had described a stripper doing a pole dance, moving up and down it like a caterpillar—but the translator had the stripper holding onto a "tube" that was moving up and down like a caterpillar! You could excuse the translator for being unfamiliar with stripper poles, but not with being so clueless about Spanish-language subjects and verbs. José was bewildered. Wasn't the United States the richest, most powerful nation on Earth? Then how could it have such incompetent professional literary translators?

I remember pondering that question, and the simple answer that occurred to me.

"It's because we're the nation we are, so rich and powerful," I told José, "that we have such incompetent translators."

After all, he was one of those rare foreign authors who actually sells his book in the United States, it being a known fact that no other country publishes fewer books in translation—defiant monolingualism can sometimes seem an essential aspect of our national literary *carácter*. Everyone knows that if people in other countries want to do business with us, they have to do it in our language. If the leaders of foreign countries want to negotiate with us, they have to do it in our language, too. A country that speaks to the world only in its own language and describes reality to itself only in its own language will be able to convince itself of anything. Sometimes that may be a recipe for muscular triumph, and sometimes for tragedy. But it's obvious, José—translators aren't what made America great.

Once you possess another language, your sense of reality changes—it's as simple as being able to connect to the Internet and read, say, what people in Mexico are saying about the immigration issue. Suddenly the world seems twice as large, and twice as peopled, and more interesting than it did before.

The summer after my junior year in college, in 1976, I invited some of my college buddies down to Guatemala, where we could travel around a bit and stay with my family. Four of us drove from Ann Arbor in my friend's Ford Mustang. It was an important trip in many ways, but there is one incident that especially haunts me. We were out walking in Guatemala City one night, on deserted streets near the Parque España traffic rotary. A VW Thing with four guys our age pulled up, and they asked us in Spanish if we knew where there was a good disco. We climbed aboard and went bombing around the city in futile and soon forgotten search for that disco. Eight of us jammed into a VW Thing, smoking the most potent pot I'd ever had. But the universal stoner's language is not quite comparable to the Language of Diplomacy. With my fractured Spanish, I divined that they were college students like us, but from neighboring El Salvador. The Salvadoran Army had stormed and occupied their campus, massacred a bunch of students, and they had fled in their VW Thing to Guatemala City, to get out of harm's way, I guess, and to just hang out.

I didn't know anything else about them, and even less about the political situation in El Salvador. I didn't know if they were at all political or what they really thought about anything or what their lives were like, and my Spanish wasn't good enough to find out. I didn't suspect, of course, that within a few years, Guatemala City, El Salvador, and most of Central America would be engulfed in violence and war. And I had no inkling that I'd spend so much of the rest of my 20s there, covering the wars as a freelance journalist, working at my first novel, and just living and learning. I only knew that there seemed to be something deeply daring and wild and intensely alive about those guys in their VW Thing, and that some of that was rubbing off on us as we charged around those dark, mostly deserted streets that night, the cool mountain tropical air in our faces and hair, making our shirts flap. After we'd ridden around awhile, they let us off and drove away. I like to think that one of those Salvadoran kids was like a version of my old lost self. We'd met, and smoked some pot. But we hadn't really been able to talk—a door slammed shut on all my curiosity.

If we met today, communication wouldn't be a problem. I'm a fairly fluent Spanish speaker again, just like when I was four. For years my mother and I have spoken only Spanish to each other. To get my Spanish back took a long time and enormous commitment. To borrow a certain literary metaphor, it was like constructing my own garden of forking paths that I can follow back into the past, to a place where that lost boy and I were never separated, and forward into a familiar landscape where two separate countries comprise one.

FRANCISCO GOLDMAN (Boston, Massachusetts; 1954-) is the author of four books and numerous pieces of journalism for publications such as *Harper's*, *The New Yorker*, and *The New York Review of Books*. His first two novels, *The Long Night of White Chickens* and *The Ordinary Seaman*, were finalists for the PEN/Faulkner Award. His third novel was *The Divine Husband*. His newest title is *The Art of Political Murder: Who Didn't Kill the Bishop?*, a nonfiction account of the 1998 murder of Guatemala's Bishop Juan José Gerardi. Goldman teaches at Trinity College in Hartford, Connecticut.

The Special English Girls

— BY GIOCONDA BELLI —

THE FIRST IMAGE MY MEMORY sees is of the old and lush bread-fruit tree that grew at the center of the Nicaraguan schoolyard. The school was run by Catholic nuns. Dressed in their long purple robes with headdresses that framed their faces, the nuns appeared to glide down the halls shepherding the girls to their classrooms. I must have been six or seven when I was registered for the Special English program. On the first day of the school year, my mother dropped me off at the school entrance sounding quite excited and content at having had the foresight to sign me up for the new course the nuns had instituted that year. Dressed in my uniform, pleated blue checkered skirt and white shirt, I remember feeling anointed for a unique mission. We, the Special English girls, were going to be set apart from the rest of the class. We were going to study every subject in English in a separate classroom.

The room was located in one corner of the school's monumental building, a veritable fortress of knowledge rising on the shores of Lake Managua. Until it was destroyed by an earthquake in 1972, it always looked as if it had been recently built because the nuns never painted its cement walls. Only the wooden doors broke the monotony of its gray surfaces.

The English teacher's name was Ruth. Miss Ruth. At first sight I decided she resembled Margot Fonteyn, the English prima ballerina who was one of my heroes. I often dreamt of being a ballet dancer in one of the grand theaters of the world. One of my favorite pastimes was to close my eyes while listening to a recording of *Swan Lake* or *The Nutcracker* and imagine myself dressed in a tutu and point shoes, sliding as weightless as a feather, possessed by the music.

I liked the fact that Miss Ruth carried herself like a ballet dancer. She was petite, her back was always straight, and she had short black hair, large dark eyes, and a slightly curved nose. She was not beautiful, but she was smart and had the gift of authority. She explained the rules of the game to us that day: within those walls nothing but English would be spoken. On the blackboard she had written the sentences we would need to ask permission to go to the bathroom or to speak. She had also written the words *thank you* and *please*. What she proposed might sound difficult to us, she said, but we were the Special English girls, the ones chosen to prove that the new program could work out. The nuns were going to follow our progress very closely to make sure we could rise to the challenge.

Her words touched the budding sense of pride we all carried within and like a chosen people we set ourselves to learn English with all the energy we could muster at our young age.

When I arrived home that afternoon, my mother was anxiously waiting to find out what my first day of classes had been like. I repeated the few words I had learned, which made her quite happy. To know English was so important, she said as she set off to speak about one of her favorite subjects: the years she had spent in Philadelphia, at Ravenhill Academy, learning English and finishing high school. That experience was my mother's pride and joy. She would endlessly repeat the stories of her happy times there and the many things she had learned at that boarding school run by nuns of the same order that ran Managua's school. At Ravenhill, my mother had shared the same classroom with Grace Kelly. Mother prided herself in having been invited to that princely wedding, a distinction which gained such notoriety in our small country that it was reported in the newspapers. She kept the clippings in her scrapbook. Judging from the way she told those stories, it seemed she attributed her good fortune to her knowledge of English and her study of English literature. I felt very close to my mother that day, as if the classes I was taking were the first step toward that larger world my mother could describe so well and where, I suspect, she would rather have lived.

The Special English classes also raised my stature before my siblings. They were always asking me how to say this or that. What I didn't know, I would make up. I remember when Christmas came around and one of them asked me how to say it, since the word seemed impossible to pronounce in Spanish. I responded with aplomb: "Chirismismas."

The realization that English was the key to accessing other perceptions and flavors of the world came to me some years later, after our group of Special English girls graduated into adolescence. Miss Ruth was substituted by a different teacher, a much younger woman. Before she became our teacher, I had seen her around the school. She was very beautiful and almost always dressed in white. Her very fair skin was enhanced by her long, dark hair, which she wore tied in a loose, low bun. On one occasion, while I was walking down the street with my mother, I had seen her walking ahead of us, her boyfriend's arm over her shoulders. They had seemed to me to be very much in love. They were smiling and kissing, and I was mesmerized at seeing in real life a scene that, according to me, existed only in movies or novels.

In her role as teacher, however, María Mercedes was initially quite serious and strict. She would give long and boring dictations in class, and I was beginning to strip her of the romantic aura I had bestowed on her. Then one day, she went up to the teacher's podium and said she would read some stories to us. Miss María Mercedes had a soft and well modulated voice. As soon as she started to read, her words captured me. If I am not mistaken, the story was about a terminally ill young woman who watched a beautiful tree of green and abundant foliage through her window. When summer ebbed and the leaves of the tree began to fall, the young woman became convinced that once the tree lost its last leaf, she would die. As I listened to the story, I felt I was the young sick girl waiting for that last leaf to fall; I felt that the breadfruit tree at the center of the schoolyard, whose leaves I could see from the classroom window, was the tree that would signal the end of her life. When the story ended, I had tears in my eyes and the story floated in my imagination like a brilliant jewel.

The beauty of that text, however, paled in comparison to the one that Miss María Mercedes read in the following class. It was the story of a couple, very much in love but very poor. When Christmas comes around, husband and wife have to use their imagination to come up with a way to give each other presents. The young wife has a marvelous head of hair and decides to sell her hair to buy the husband a gold chain for an old watch that he treasures. When the husband arrives home with his present, he sees she has cut her hair and lets out a cry. It turns out he had bought a set of combs she had seen and wished for at a store. She then shows him her present, the gold chain. In turn, he tells her that he sold his watch to buy her the combs.

As I listened to the story in the classroom, time came to a halt. With no effort, my mind traveled to the young couple's living room and I became an invisible witness of their mutual generosity. To this day I can still see them as if instead of having heard their tale read aloud, I had been present in that room with them.

It was then I realized that English was a language that could reveal to me an unknown world that was lost in the translations I had read of English authors. I made a commitment to learn English as best as I could.

The following year I left Nicaragua to go to a boarding school in Madrid. I spent the summer with a wonderful English family in Ixworth, a quaint town east of London. When I turned 16, like my mother, I also lived in Philadelphia, at Ravenhill Academy, while I went to advertising school downtown.

As I came to have greater command of the English language, I dared to tread further afield and read my favorite writers in the original. Nothing I have read, however, has equaled the sense of discovery I experienced when I grasped for the first time the emotions and sounds a different language can evoke. It seems I can still hear the echo of María Mercedes's voice, flowing through the tropical heat in a gray Nicaraguan classroom that no longer exists.

Author **GIOCONDA BELLI** (Managua, Nicaragua; 1948-) has written *The Scroll of Seduction: A Novel*, and *The Country under My Skin: A Memoir of Love and War*, among other books. Between 1978 and 1986 she held high-level positions in the Sandinista National Liberation Front and Nicaragua's government. Belli has won numerous literary awards throughout Europe and the Americas.

From Montevideo to Saginaw in One Easy Lesson

— NANDO PARRADO —

I WAS BORN IN MONTEVIDEO, URUGUAY, so my native language is Spanish. My mother, though, was Russian, having emigrated to Uruguay with her family at the tender age of 16. As a result, I also learned some Russian as a child.

My first contact with the English language, remarkably enough, came through *National Geographic* magazine. As with many families in the civilized world, someone through the generations had subscribed to *National Geographic*. Since I was very small, probably four or five years old, the sight of those yellow magazines stacked in a bookshelf in our house always got my attention. Once I started to browse them, I became instantly absorbed by the fantastic photographs of faraway places, strange civilizations, exotic animals, and different ethnics. When I started to go to kindergarten and then in first grade, I also began learning how to read and write Spanish. But whenever I went back to the yellow magazines, I saw that the letters and words were arranged in a different way. I asked my father why I couldn't read them. "It is English, Nando. It is another language, spoken by people from faraway places," he said.

From that moment on, I always went to him whenever I was looking at a *National Geographic* so that he could translate what the photo captions said. My father could read English reasonably well. He had taken some classes in the language when he was younger and then read everything that he could in English to improve his abilities. His spoken English and pronunciation was not as good—but he traveled extensively in the United States and never had any problems.

I decided that I should learn English so I could read those yellow magazines by myself. Fortunately, I was enrolled as a student in the Stella Maris School, which was a branch of the Christian Brothers of Ireland, and they started to teach us English even in our first year in primary school. Every afternoon we had two hours of English, and during that time it was forbidden to speak Spanish, even during the breaks between classes. I was six or seven and I was already learning English.

With my desire to read *National Geographic*, plus the car magazines that my father was buying from the United States—*Car & Driver*, *Sports Car Graphic*, and others—I became quite a good student. It was the only subject in school in which I ever got straight A's—I was always swimming between B's and C's!

I loved being able to understand a different language by myself, and once I had mastered *NG* and the car magazines, I started reading adventure books in English such as *Twenty-Thousand Leagues under the Sea* and *The Voyages of Marco Polo*. By the time I was 16, my mother had enrolled me in an exchange student program, which, if I was selected, would mean I'd go to the United States for a year to study and, hopefully, graduate from a high school there.

Great news! I was selected as one of the exchange students! With apprehension and a little fear, late one December night I boarded the plane that took me and six others to the United States. I was assigned to a family that lived in Saginaw, Michigan, and I arrived there on December 25, 1966. What a shock—what a cold climate! I had seen snow before only in pictures, and I arrived there in the middle of the winter. Now *that* was a grand experience. But the best experience, and the one I had dreamed of, was the opportunity to keep on improving my English. I knew that nobody would speak Spanish in Saginaw and I would be on my own.

I had two North American brothers, Pat and Bob, and I was enrolled in Saginaw High with them. This was such a great experience. As a South American with a strange accent, girls flocked around me, and they taught me a lot about English and the American way of life. I learned words, slang, and behavior that was completely strange to me, but that spoke to the American culture and how teenagers could vary so much in taste and customs. The drive-in movie was the place to go on weekends, and I became an avid fan—although I must have seen only a few of them! I also played on the school's tennis squad, traveling around the state, playing against other high school teams. This also gave me confidence and the chance to speak with a lot of different people.

The years went by and I started working and developing my own life in several fields, especially in hardware stores and in the media. These businesses required a lot of international travel, seeking new products at fairs and conventions, where the international language was obviously English. I have become so focused on the English language that, when I am in the States, I even think in English now. I often surprise myself saying in my mind things such as, "I should park over there," or "Oh my God, look at that." All those common expressions that I might have been thinking in Spanish, my mind brings out of its English folder and sparks the brain to start in that language.

The English language has probably been one of the most important things in my life. It has allowed me to travel without restrictions, to communicate with people all over the world, to conduct business, and to make new friends. It has been great.

But where it all started is so important to me—with *National Geographic*, because now, some 50 years later, I have become a well-known television host and producer in my country. Through my business contacts, and because of my English, I started buying television programs, and one of those is the *National Geographic Specials* series. I have been presenting them on television every

Saturday for the last 24 years. Those yellow magazines really did their work!

NANDO PARRADO (Montevideo, Uruguay; 1949-) is the author of *Miracle in the Andes: 72 Days on the Mountain and My Long Trek Home,* an account of the horrifying 1972 airplane crash high in the Andes in which the author was a survivor and eventually a savior. Parrado, now a successful business-man and television personality in his home country, gives inspirational talks to organizations throughout the world on leadership, loyalty, and perseverance.

English: My Passport to Poetry and Theatre, Science and Life

– WALTER MERCADO –

MY MOTHER, MY GREATEST inspiration, spoke English all the time. She was born in Barcelona, Spain, and traveled around the world, visiting England and the United States for her scholarly preparation. Because of her influence, my family spoke English most of the time so we could get acquainted with the language. She loved English poetry, and together in my youth she and I would read and memorize sonnets and poems written by Robert Burns, Henry Wadsworth Longfellow, Elizabeth Barrett Browning, and Edgar Allan Poe. I read works by writers such as William Shakespeare and Somerset Maugham.

My first English teachers were my mother and my aunt María Luisa Salinas. Aunt María Luisa taught English in elementary schools in the rural area of Ponce, Puerto Rico. When I entered school there, I was the best student in English. When I moved to San Juan, the schools considered me gifted because of my English. As a teenager I read Emily and Charlotte Brontë as a hobby, and Christopher Marlowe in the original English. Charles Dickens, Walt Whitman, and John Steinbeck were favorites, as were Tennessee Williams, Truman Capote, and Ann Rice.

For me, English is the best way of communicating my ideas. I have read the language voraciously all my life. Among my favorite books were the *Fairy Tales* of Hans Christian Andersen and volumes by Oscar Wilde.

After I graduated from high school I acted in many plays such as *Anne of the Thousand Days* by Maxwell Anderson, the drama *Hands across the Sea*, and Arthur Miller's *The Crucible*, all in English, with the Puerto Rico Little Theater, the Ateneo Puertorriqueño, and Teatro Tapia of Old San Juan. I have performed on television in London. I even had the golden opportunity to audition with the Twenty Players of London. I landed a bit part in *Joan of Arc*. It was a wonderful experience to be around actors who spoke the language so elegantly.

My best acting teacher was Sanford Meisner in New York City when I was 20 years old. He taught me the art of projecting myself artistically in English, a skill I have used ever since. I gave seminars and acting classes at my own academy, Walter's Actors Studio, in Santurce, Puerto Rico, between 1960 and 1970.

My manager, Bill Bakula, insisted I take classes to polish my Spanish accent to a more universal one. Among my teachers in New York City was Dorothy Sarnoff, who taught me about preparation and performance in English.

Deco Drive, an entertaining daily English-language television program in Miami, offered me a contract giving astrological predictions. At this time I keep up my English by speaking with friends in the United States and Great Britain.

I have had many opportunities to use my English on programs hosted by Sally Jesse Raphael, Howard Stern, and Regis Philbin. One of my most difficult experiences in English took place when I was interviewed for two hours in the Middle East with two translators by my side, one who spoke Hebrew and the other Arabic. The translators were very distracting and affected my concentration, but it was an excellent and unexpected lesson in expression.

I've written all of my books in English, after which they've been translated into Spanish and Portuguese. As you can see, I am a Puerto Rican with deep respect and love for the English language.

WALTER MERCADO (Ponce, Puerto Rico; 1932-) has gained international fame through his theatrical televised daily horoscope readings. In his youth he attended pharmacy school but soon turned to acting. He appeared in numerous soap operas in Puerto Rico and eventually adopted astrology as his medium. Mercado, a Pisces, appeared in the movie *Chasing Papi* wearing his well-known colorful cape. He is the author of *Beyond the Horizon* and other titles.

When I Was a Little Cuban Boy

– RICHARD BLANCO –

O José can you see...that's how I sang it, when I was
a *cubanito* in Miami, and *América* was some country
in the glossy pages of my history book, someplace
way north, everyone white, cold, perfect. *This Land
Is my Land*, so why didn't I live there, in a brick house
with a fireplace, a chimney with curlicues of smoke.
I wanted to wear breeches and stockings to my *chins*,
those black pilgrim shoes with shinny gold buckles.
I wanted to eat yams with the Indians, shake hands
with *los negros*, and dash through snow I'd never seen
in a one-horse hope-n-say? I wanted to speak in British,
say really smart stuff like *fours core and seven years ago*
or *one country under God, in the visible*. I wanted to see
that land with no palm trees, only the strange sounds
of flowers like petunias, peonies, impatience, waiting
to walk through a door someday, somewhere in God
Bless America and say, *Lucy, I'm home, honey. I'm home.*

Poet **RICHARD BLANCO** (Madrid, Spain; 1968-) is the author of
City of a Hundred Fires and *Directions to the Beach of the
Dead*. Blanco, who is widely published in literary journals,
has won many awards, including a Residency Fellowship from
the Virginia Center for the Creative Arts.

part two

The English have no respect for their language, and will not teach their children to speak it. They spell it so abominably that no man can teach himself what it sounds like.

—George Bernard Shaw, *Pygmalion*

Yellow Magazine

— ELENA PONIATOWSKA —

MY GRANDMOTHER WAS AMERICAN. She came from Stockton, California, and her name was Elizabeth Sperry Crocker. Although my family name is Polish, the Poniatowski family has been French for nearly 400 years because the Poniatowskis were expelled from Poland after Stanislas Augustus Poniatowski was made king (the last king of Poland) in 1764 by Catherine the Great. Poniatowski was her first lover, and we keep his love letters that cry out: "I don't want to be king, I want to be in your bed." But he was a very good king. Prince Joseph Poniatowski was one of Napoleon's Maréchals de France; he threw himself with his army into the Elster River rather than surrender to the Russians. Michel Poniatowski was secretary of state during the mandate of Valéry Giscard d'Estaing. My mother's family was Mexican, but she was born in Paris, as was my grandmother. They had to leave Mexico because in 1910 the Mexican Revolution took their lands away.

Paris is where my parents met and, with my grandparents, André Poniatowski and Elizabeth Sperry Crocker, shared the enormous house in Rue Berton where my sister Kitzia and I were raised. The Poniatowskis were a close family and my uncle Casimir and his wife Anne also lived on the corner of Rue Berton. My grandmother spoke such bad French that I thought I was always hearing English, or maybe she spoke English with a slight French accent and tried to pass it off as French. She called my father Johnny.

Every night, after dinner, my sister and I used to sit at her side while she read *National Geographic* magazine to us. There were piles of this yellow magazine in the house. It was the first magazine I ever saw in my life. I was seven years old. When our grandmother learned that my mother was going to take us to Mexico because of the war spreading across Europe, she used *National Geographic* as a weapon against our departure. There were photographs of Africans with bones on top of their heads, ears pierced by knives and lips like plates, and she exclaimed, "You see, children, this is Mexico." When we arrived in Mexico we were sure we would be eaten up.

Elizabeth Sperry Crocker also told us that Benjamin Franklin was our ancestor, that William Crocker had built the Museum of Modern Art in San Francisco, now called the Crocker Museum, and that her own father had started the Chihuahua Pacific Railway whose locomotive can be seen in Sacramento. But most of all she asked, when we came back from the WC, in her American French: "*Avez-vous fait le grand chose ou le petit chose?*" When I was told later in school that Napoleon had done great things, I wondered which one.

I didn't really learn English until I went to a wonderful school in Mexico City when I was 11 years old: the Windsor School, directed by an Englishwoman, Mrs. Hart. Now that I look back, I realize how good the school was. Half of every morning Mrs. Hart gave us English lessons, and I never had a better or a more severe teacher. We were taught to count in pounds, shillings, and pence. Every morning we sang "God Save the Queen," so we learned to respect Elizabeth II more than the Mexican president. Because of her love for England, Mrs. Hart made us citizens of the world.

Later, when my father came back from the war, my sister and I were sent to a Sacred Heart convent in the Torresdale section of Philadelphia. The neighborhood seemed to be a very small town then, where there was only a prison, an insane asylum, our convent, and a train station that had a small drugstore where we could drink ice cream sodas. There was nothing to do during those years except to learn English and study in English and pray in English and ask forgiveness for our sins in English and play hockey in English. (One of the great triumphs of our team before I became a very bad left wing was that our Catholic Convent of the Sacred Heart Eden Hall had won a hockey game against Ravenhill, where Grace Kelly had studied.) But still, one student, designated a "Child of Mary" for her character and good behavior, managed to elope with a convict from the prison. No one ever knew how she met him, but the fact is that she became pregnant. I used to hear her in the dormitory bump herself against the floor in an extraordinary gymnastic because she said she was getting fat. In truth, she was growing visibly pregnant and hoped her exercises would induce a miscarriage.

English was my grandmother's language and my father's language. My mother also spoke English, and my sister married an American. In Mexico I don't have the opportunity to speak it often, but I love to listen to it as I consider it beautiful, especially when I read Virginia Woolf. It is an extraordinary language, and when I translate Spanish into English, I realize how concise and truthful it is, because Spanish says with many words what English says with very few.

I am grateful for having been able to read Elizabeth Barrett Browning's "How do I love thee? Let me count the ways" that every young girl wants to say to her boyfriend. As the maid in Shakespeare's *Twelfth Night*, I remember pouring and pouring big glasses of wine on stage, which in reality was tainted water, while I kept giggling and flirting with some of my tall and fat roommates who played very healthy drinkers. I am also happy to have been a Child of Mary, a distinction that allowed me to enter first in the chapel instead of going in with the first-grade students because I was so short. The nuns that taught us were friendly and funny, and accepted us as we were, children full of illusions and good will.

Maybe I will die in English because of all the prayers taught to me during those years and because I was told that the Virgin, Holy Mary Mother of God, would come and pull me to heaven by my Child of Mary blue ribbon and that I would sit on a cloud next to God and all my loved ones.

The writing career of **ELENA PONIATOWSKA** (Paris, France; 1932-) spans two generations and includes *Las Soldaderas: Women of the Mexican Revolution*, *Here's to You, Jesusa!*, and *Massacre in Mexico*. She has published personality profiles of Tina Modotti (*Tinísima*) and Diego Rivera (*Dear Diego*). Among Poniatowska's many awards are a Guggenheim Fellowship and an Emeritus Fellowship from Mexico's National Council of Culture and Arts. Her full name is Hélène Elizabeth Louise Amelie Paula Dolores Poniatowska Amor.

The Learning Curve

– RUBÉN MARTÍNEZ –

IT WAS LONG BEFORE the debates over bilingual education or English Only or whether a hyphenated American was a real American. Before we knew who César Chávez was, before black or brown or red or yellow power. It was the time of JFK, and the Russians and the Beatles were about to conquer us. No one knew the name of the president of Mexico or where El Salvador was. Assimilation was assumed. And my parents, without slogans, without following leaders charismatic or demagogic or otherwise, without proclaiming themselves "Chicano" (and certainly not "Chicana/o"), decided that I, their first child and American citizen by birth, would speak Spanish before English.

There was indeed a culture war raging in early 1960s America, but its terms were literally black and white. Dr. Martin Luther King Jr. spread his arms wide above the reflecting pool on the National Mall to tell us that one day black children and white children would join hands together—but there was no question what language they would speak to one another. My family's rites of language took place in the shadow of the civil rights movement—both related to and utterly disconnected from it in the vast realm of immigrant America.

Actually my parents didn't discuss the issue at the time. Spanish was the undisputed lingua franca in our sparkling new house on Hollyvista Avenue in the hills east of Hollywood. We lived in a middle-class neighborhood dominated by English (save for the Persian family a few doors down and a bit of Yiddish in the Jewish households). The minute my parents stepped out the front door, English took over.

So my first few years were spent mostly inside the House of Spanish. I uttered my first intelligible words (*mamá, papá, agua*) in the year 1963. My babbling turned to words, words to phrases—desire molded into consonants and vowels and accented syllables. *Quiero leche. ¡Quiero más! Te quiero, mamá.* I heard others, I heard myself. Language created time, which made relationships possible, and these existed in different rhythms. Formal: *Usted* (my parents speaking to my grandparents, to strangers, and even to each other). Informal: *Tú* (my parents speaking to their siblings and cousins, to friends, to me). Hierarchy. So Latin American—so very colonial. Americans take pride in the democratic vistas of their English, in its inherent equal protection clause. You can address the blue-collar laborer and the president with the same pronoun, the same expletives. (Then again, it can be great fun to combine the formal address with terrible vulgarity in Spanish.)

I have been asked to write about how I learned English, and I realize that I am telling you how I learned Spanish. I assume that I occupy a slightly different position than most of the other contributors to this volume. This is not an immigrant tale—it is the tale of the child of immigrants, that is, an American one.

There was no question that I would speak Spanish first, because I was the first child born to a mostly immigrant family. I say "mostly" because, although my mother had arrived in the States from El Salvador only a few years before my birth, my father had actually been born here to immigrant parents from Mexico and was raised on both sides of the border. Pop spoke perfect Spanish and English—English in the world of work beyond the house on Hollyvista, and Spanish inside it because that was the language of my parents' courtship (which in turn was the case because it was the language of my mother's heart).

By the time I was born, Mom spoke English quite well, but it made no sense for her to speak it to me. Ironically, American English for our young family was more formal than Spanish. English was the language for bank transactions, to address men in suits, what Walter Cronkite spoke when every evening he informed us of people we didn't know personally but whose lives had a great impact on ours. Walter Cronkite is an *Usted*. As a matter of fact, from the immigrant point of view, all gringos are Usted—strangers. And compared to Spanish, English is always a little abstract. You (I'm thinking in Spanish now—Tú) can't imagine it whispered in your ear. English can be exciting, it can be fun or chic—but only with difficulty can it encompass tragedy or love, or the tragedy of love. (I think of Cronkite again: announcing JFK's assassination live on television a few months after I was born, he can barely utter the words.) Consider the gravitas of *te amo* compared to the playful but ultimately bland package of "I love you."

I am two years old. I exist almost exclusively inside the vowels of Spanish (which dominate it as English is shaped by consonants). More, I exist mostly in the Spanish my mother speaks—Salvadoran Spanish, which includes yet another pronoun, *Vos*, a diminutive of the ultimate Spanish formalism (*Vosotros*), but which in most of Central America (and Argentina) actually functions as the most casual address. Mom sings my lullabies in Spanish (*Los tres cochinitos están en la cama…*). She loves poetry and she recites it in Spanish (*Verde verde, que te quiero verde…*). My parents are young and in love, and I hear them coo to each other in Spanish (their terms of endearment for each other are *pingüino* and *pingüina*—male and female penguins).

All the while, English is waiting for me in the wings—a madman, a conqueror, a liberator with an axe. English will be my first fall.

I first hear it in the occasional anglicism or full-on English words inserted into conversation otherwise conducted in Spanish. How we say *chainear* for the verb "to shine." Or, around April 15, how immigrants say *income tax* in accented English (they would never think to search for the translation in Spanish; the American taxman is an Usted).

And on television, of course. It is a big wooden Zenith in the living room, and it is on every evening. Through it comes Walter Cronkite's voice. It is a friendly tongue, and it is pinched. It is democratic, and it is nervous. It is young, and the rest of the world is old. (My young parents are older than Walter Cronkite when they speak in Spanish.)

I am three years old, and I know how to turn on the television. It is early in the morning. Pop has just left for work, but my mother is still in bed. The box makes a loud buzzing sound when I push the power button, and when I turn the dial to change stations it goes clunk-clunk. Last night, the box spoke English. But this morning, it is speaking Spanish, through a woman that looks not unlike my mother, with tall arched hair and heavily penciled eyebrows and lips that shine in the studio lights. *Escuche bien*, she says. Listen carefully. *Repite*. Repeat. She is addressing me as an Usted. Now I am old. It is a Spanish lesson. Is it for native Spanish speakers? For gringos headed to Acapulco? My parents do not recall the show, nor does anyone else. It was the first inkling I had that Spanish could exist out in the world beyond the front door.

Clunk-clunk.

Now the box is talking cowboy. "Howdy, buckaroos!" gushes the man in hat, boots, and spurs, host of a children's program called *Buckaroo 500*. Soon I will have cowboys-and-injuns plastic figurines. I will wear cow-print chaps and sit on a pony for my Western portrait. I am now a brown cowboy, and I speak a patois of Spanish and English with neologisms that fall somewhere in between.

I arrive at Hilltop Nursery School, the only Hispanophone, the only brown cowboy. I gurgle my special language to the other kids. They laugh, point fingers. My gregarious demeanor gives way to a wary quiet. Except that I take to screaming when my mother drops me off, causing great scenes. My parents devise a strategy to keep me from becoming a nursery school dropout—they ask my grandfather to take me instead. He drives a big-finned Cadillac and doesn't speak a word of English. Somehow holding his hand at the entryway to Hilltop reassures me. He is releasing me into another language. I will speak the future with it. Grandfather will remain in the past. Our conversation will end.

Now the language crashes down all around me. It comes in the voices of my nursery school cohort, in the Motown hits on the radio, in the raspy voice of our wonderful octogenarian neighbor on Hollyvista, Mrs. Prophet, a woman whose pale blue eyes had seen much of the world and who helped open mine to it. There are more westerns on television. My father reads me bedtime stories; I say goodnight to the moon in English.

Kindergarten. I speak English at least as well as Spanish by now. Again, I am in a classroom surrounded by kids weaned on English. Kids who've already learned, or will shortly, that the word *Mexican* is interchangeable with "wetback" or "beaner" or "greaser." I will show them that I am not a Mexican. I will speak to them in their language—it's mine now—better than they speak to me. I will defend myself with it, use it as a weapon if necessary. I read, I write, I speak in English with tremendous energy. I am holding onto language for dear life, instinctually believing that it can work some magic against history, against the color of my skin and the ring of my surname in a town as WASP-y as L.A. was when I was growing up. (Over the course of the last 40 years, Spanish has utterly reconquered it; English is now the dialect of the minority, Spanish the language of ambition.)

I am telling you that growing up in a town that hated Mexicans and the Spanish language turned me into a writer of English.

Which language I write to tell the story of immigrants like my parents and grandparents in America. Which language I write to speak of rupture and synthesis—the constant contraries of immigrant life.

This is how I learned English, but I must tell you that I did not "forget" Spanish. The basic vocabulary and structure that I learned as a very young child stayed with me and grew into a mature tongue, in large part due to numerous trips to visit my mother's family in El Salvador in the 1960s and '70s and later living in Latin America for several years. I do not speak or write it as well as English, but I have considered it one of my greatest responsibilities to cultivate it. I was born in Spanish, after all. History resides in language, and I know that my family has brought from Spanish into English a vast legacy. I also know that English has had an enormous impact on Spanish. The melodrama of this relationship would best be described in Spanish.

In a few weeks, my wife will give birth to twin daughters. We have often talked about what we'd like their experience of language to be like, even as we admit that whatever grand trilingual designs we may have for them (they will also speak French, or perhaps an Asian language), there is little we can do to avoid the power of the world beyond our home to shape their tongues. Last night, I recited poetry to them, having learned that at this stage of pregnancy their sense of hearing is fully developed.

I read them Neruda.

And I read them Whitman.

RUBÉN MARTÍNEZ (Los Angeles, California; 1962-) is the author of *Crossing Over: A Mexican Family on the Migrant Trail; The Other Side: Notes from the New L.A., Mexico City, and Beyond;* and *The New Americans,* the companion book to a 2004 PBS miniseries. Over the years his many outlets have included *LA Weekly,* NPR, PBS, the *New York Times,* and *Mother Jones* magazine. Martínez, also a poet and rock musician, is the winner of a Lannan Foundation fellowship and currently holds the Fletcher Jones Chair in Literature & Writing at Loyola Marymount University in Los Angeles.

A Subtitled Life

– ENRIQUE FERNÁNDEZ –

OF COURSE, I ALWAYS knew English. Just like, since my youth, I have known French and Italian. I know Italian, the Italian of Antonioni. I know the French of Truffaut–if I have an accent in my very, very limited French, it's Jean-Pierre Leaud's. And I have always known the English spoken by Wayne, Bogart, Curtis, Douglas, Brando, Mason, Olivier–though the fact that they each spoke it differently, the product of backgrounds etched in speech, erased because of ethnic shame and commercial intent or cultivated because they were profitable, eluded me for years.

Give me subtitles and I'll give you basic language comprehension.

Reading subtitles has nothing to do with reading a work in translation, that necessary evil. I know nothing of the basic structure of Russian nor do I know its cognates, except for a handful of Cold War words that sneaked into the international vocabulary, mostly through–what else?–the movies. So when I read Tolstoy, I was reading Tolstoy's translators. When I watch a subtitled movie, I am hearing and reading at the same time, a skill I acquired involuntarily at a very early age. Nothing, short of unmediated language, comes closer to instant understanding.

Hearing Marie Riviere in Eric Rohmer's *Autumn Song* say, provocatively, that she is a winemaker (and the French, particularly the French in Rohmer's films, always manage to be sexually provocative no matter what they're saying), I know she is saying that because I have, in a flash, read it. So I can savor the way she puckers her mouth while her eyes sparkle and she s-l-o-w-l-y enunciates *viticultrice*, the feminine word, full of seduction, inviting, stroking the male imagination to the pleasures of the French bed. That's understanding with perks.

The American movies of my Havana childhood were not lacking in sexual invitation. There was Marilyn Monroe in *The Seven Year Itch*. A male imagination didn't need to have even reached puberty to get that. For Marilyn wasn't just puckering her mouth. She was puckering her whole body.

Did I understand everything? I was a kid. I didn't even know exactly what Marilyn was puckering up for. But I knew it was for something.

So when I moved, at the age of 13, from a Spanish-speaking country to this English-speaking one, I foresaw no problem. That I could not understand some of my interlocutors nor they understand me was puzzling. Coming from a sophisticated metropolis to the Gulf Coast of Florida, I knew this noncommunication was related to underdevelopment. Obviously not mine.

Speaking—as opposed to understanding—English was almost the same. What came out of my mouth and reached my ear was perfect English. It could not have been. That's how it sounded to me. An auditory hallucination, not unlike one I experienced, years later, when, under the influence of actual hallucinogens, I picked up a guitar at a party and played a flamenco riff that sounded to my ears like Sabicas, the master of those pre–Paco de Lucía years. Since everyone around me was just as stoned, it sounded like Sabicas to them, too. *¡Olé!*

Did my English improve from those days of early adolescence? It must have, but you couldn't ask me. I heard the same perfect sounds regardless of how long I'd been making them. So when someone would comment on my "accent," I was (almost) insulted. Who do you take me for, Desi Arnaz? I said inside my head, knowing that, rationally, I probably had an accent of some sort. Still, as far as I knew, I sounded like a good old boy, or an Eastern Seaboard intellectual, an L.A. entertainment-industry hipster, or, for that matter, like that curious urban beast, a "Latino," whose accent was of foreign descent but certainly homegrown in the U.S.A.—more on that later. It all depended on the circumstances.

For years I worked with language learning, but in the opposite direction. I taught college Spanish. From that experience I found out that a foreign language can be learned and that some people can learn it, while others can't no matter how hard they try. Finally, it all depends on your attitude.

The love/hate relationship between Spanish and English boils down to history. Hate with extreme prejudice is war, and that dysfunctional Spanish/English relationship had two peak moments: the Spanish Armada and the Spanish-American War. In both cases, English speakers sank Spanish ships, and in both cases Spanish speakers lost the battle to English speakers. We, the children of those empires, still bear the scars of those wars.

How can you feel good about the language of your enemy? That hinges on your enemy's powers of seduction.

As I said, I learned English at a classic seductive scene: the movies—just like the French critics-turned-filmmakers of the *nouvelle vague*, just like the Latin American novelists of el boom. But I got an extra kick those slightly older generations never did. Rock 'n' roll. I learned some of my English from Elvis Presley, thankyouverymuch. Singing like him, too. Like so many who came of age when I did, I can turn up my shirt collar, swing my hips, and do an Elvis impersonation, though I'd never make it in Vegas.

Listening to, singing like, and worshipping at the altar of Elvis does not prepare you to understand other Tennesseans, or any Southerners for that matter, as I found out when I moved to the American South. It does not even prepare you to understand Elvis. Like most foreigners who learned to mouth American songs, I barely knew what I was saying, and half the time I was singing the wrong words.

Then, I actually heard the roots of Elvis. Among the Tampa radio stations of the 1950s, there was one that played "race" music. I took these sounds to be related to my beloved rock, still in its first phase and not too far from its R&B roots. Besides, a number of black musicians—Chuck Berry, Little Richard, Fats Domino—were in the first rock canon. But when I tuned in that station I was dumbfounded. Not only could I not understand the growling, moaning vocals of the blues, I could not differentiate them from the growling, moaning of the guitars that backed up the vocals of a genre I would learn to love a few years later.

Learning a language perfectly from the get-go in the classroom of the mass media shelters you from language in its vital rawness. It would be like learning Spanish only from watching *telenovelas*. Their stilted, formal dialogue is nothing like what you'd hear on the streets of Mexico City, Caracas, Buenos Aires, or Madrid.

Learning a language is a lifelong endeavor, and like all endeavors, as prone to improvement as it is doomed to failure. I still discover, for example, that I've been pronouncing a phoneme incorrectly all my American life. Or that I am using the wrong preposition —English has a preposition for every conceivable nuance of connection. And at one point in my life, my accent deteriorated.

After living all over the American provinces I finally made it to New York in early middle age. There I fell in with Latin American immigrants like myself, though more recently arrived, and with Cuban-Americans who, unlike myself, had spent most of their lives around each other, thus still speaking English with a marked Cuban accent. Used to aping sounds, I simply went into reverse. My English lost its Southern and Midwestern twangs; it lost its academic hauteur as well. And this time I gained a new skill. Much to my chagrin, I began to hear myself.

I sounded like a foreigner, like a Latin American immigrant, like a Latino, like a Cuban-American, like a Cuban.

Like Desi Arnaz.

But Desi loves Lucy and she loves him back. The pedagogy of desire is the best. From my years as a language teacher, I know that a foreign language is most efficiently learned in bed. Some student of mine, two or three years into Spanish, would go on a semester abroad. And she—it was usually a she—would come back completely fluent. How so? When she started telling me how she missed Carlos or Jorge, I knew.

Makes sense. The best classroom is mother's lap. In that warm, secure place, a child will learn anything, and very quickly, too. Next best—an improvement, we think after puberty—is the lap of someone we are sexually involved with. Had I stayed linked to my "own kind," as they sing in *West Side Story*, I would've never learned English as quickly or as well.

Mores had dealt me a hand. In the days before the sexual revolution, Latin girls were hard to get; they required elaborate courtship, *tallar una jeva* (to carve out a chick) in the Cuban slang of my early years. "American" girls, as we called them, were "easier" because they were, not sluts as machismo would have it, but simply more modern. In the end, all girls would be easier, as modernity moved and still moves through the world. A hormone-addled boy takes the path of least resistance. It's not that I didn't like Latin girls—in my first youth, I made no cultural distinctions when it came to sex—it's just that I didn't have the staying power to court them.

Same thing happened to those Latin girls, I learned years later, when a Cuban-American woman I flirted with—that's about as far as it went—would call me at the office and say the randiest things, only to break off giggling and add, "I've never said that in Spanish before!" I guess that is one definition of oral sex.

"Spanish is a loving tongue" goes the old cowboy song. Is it? That making love is better in Spanish is a line, a come-on, not a thesis, and some version of it must be used for cross-cultural purposes by everyone from the Inuit to the Ibo. But most definitely we learn each other's languages through intimacy: not just sex, but the unguarded closeness that comes with relationships.

Through those relationships, outdoors and in, Platonic or Priapic, in amity and in ardor, Spanglish is the language that I have been learning, unwittingly, all these years. When I talk to recently arrived

Spanish speakers or travel to a Spanish-speaking country, I must force myself to speak just Spanish. After a lifetime trying to master English, what I finally mastered, and what mastered me, was code-switching.

As Spanish invades English through demographic shifts and as English invades the world, maybe that hybrid will triumph as the dominant language. And I will be ahead of the game, fluent already, no hallucination, fluent for real in this rising tongue of the world, resident tongue of my mortal body.

ENRIQUE FERNÁNDEZ (Havana, Cuba; 1943-) wrote the "El Norte" column about New York's hipster Latino scene for the *Village Voice*, served as editor of *Más* and *Exito*, has freelanced for many magazines, and currently works as an editor and cultural critic for the *Miami Herald*.

Shaping Language

— ENRIQUE MARTÍNEZ CELAYA —

IN MADRID, WHEN MY BROTHER Carlos and I pretended to speak English, we slurred our Spanish words and spoke fast. English, for us, was a wispy buzz that carried prestige and mystery. Far away from Vietnam and Watergate, in the Spain of 1972, English was the sound of the happy children we had seen, dressed as witches and pumpkins, in an album of stamps called Children of the World.

I knew I was way ahead of my brother because my nickname, Henry, was already in English. A few years before, in Cuba, my father had taken some English lessons and bestowed upon me the honor of being, at least by name, a child of El Norte.

Carlos and I found time to slur and to affect gestures of those unknown ghoulish children as we moved from apartment to apartment in Madrid. But our version of English became a sham when we arrived in Puerto Rico. In San Juan, most children were acquainted with the real thing, and many of them had been to the United States or had family there. Nonetheless, we tried to reform our secret language, but the magic was gone. We knew we were making things up.

In school, our English skills were far behind the other students. I remember tackling Steinbeck's *Red Pony* with dread. I loved to read but there was no pleasure, no discovery, in drudging through metaphors and sentences I didn't understand. In the insecure fashion of colonial countries, one of our teachers felt that fourth grade was the right time to assign Sir Walter Scott's *Ivanhoe*. Fortunately, I was interested in archery and was able to write a one-page report on the book based only on the cover illustration and my knowledge of bows and arrows.

Those years, the seventies, are coated with memory dust and much of it came from the *English This Way* workbooks: small white pages filled with incomplete sentences, multiple choice exercises, and reading comprehension–lonely books for an unsettled time. They seemingly held the first key to love, because in my early teens all the girls I liked were masters of *English This Way*. By the end of high school, I knew enough English to do well in standardized tests and to perform the rituals of the Language Lab taught by a woman whose teased hair, to this day, I associate with English.

But my skill depended on being able to see the words on the page. Spoken English was a different matter. As I flew to Cornell for a summer program before my freshman year, I wondered about my fate. In the plane, between New York City and Ithaca, a girl my age tried to speak to me. She spoke about New York being a state of trees and open land, not just the city that everyone knew. But conveying this bucolic information took the whole flight and I interrupted dozens of times with the annoying phrase, "How do you say...?"

My first year at Cornell was the hardest. I realized that a language is not just words but a way to look at the world that includes dorm rooms, care packages from parents, brunches, work-study, knowledge of the proper clothing, and enough money for parkas. All of which were foreign to me. I stumbled through conversations, spent a great deal of time in my room or jogging, and wrote essays that were returned to me covered in red ink. I refused to sign up for the English as a Second Language type of course and instead enrolled in a freshmen seminar in introductory linguistics and the second semester something called "Writing from Experience." Those writing courses took enormous amounts of time.

Most of the English I learned that year was at dinners and casual conversations in my dorm. These lessons were awkward, and many included some humiliation or me pretending to be meeker than I was. Of those unforgettable moments none are as funny or as painful as the Constipation Story.

Ithaca has a tough climate, and I was sick quite often. I caught a cold or a flu four or five times that first year.

Throughout my freshman year I frequently told my classmates and people sitting around dining tables that I was constipated. In Spanish, *constipado* means having a cold.

One morning in my sophomore year, a friend who spoke both Spanish and English corrected my constipated mistake. I looked at him carefully. Embarrassed. I pictured a year of secret laughter and bewilderment for my bodily openness. Maybe by now, more than 20 years later, my condition is an urban legend; the constipated boy who jumped from one of those infamous Cornell bridges.

The truth is that English came slowly, imperceptibly, over a few decades. All the markers, all the stories, can't completely pinpoint how the learning happened. One day I read *Moby-Dick* and it didn't seem foreign. At Berkeley I reread Steinbeck looking at those parched California hills that I didn't understand as a kid, and the metaphors made sense.

I had thought that mastering a language was understanding its grammar and vocabulary.

But Spanish had been more than that. It had been the feeling of the poems of Miguel Hernández and Jorge Luis Borges, the music of Joan Manuel Serrat, and the gestures of my father. In a similar way, Steinbeck was those golden hills that didn't make sense in any language when all the hills I had seen were verdant and lush. The deceptive simplicity of Robert Frost or the idea of "plainness" existed in language, and the language existed in them. Learning English was learning to love the sensibility, the rustle, that connects the words.

I am still learning, and probably my English will always reflect my Spanish upbringing, not only in my accent, but also in a way of thinking, a way of wanting to use the language. My Spanish has also changed. Language, it turns out, was not something to learn but something to learn through.

The art of **ENRIQUE MARTÍNEZ CELAYA** (Palos, Cuba; 1964-) ranges from conventional oils to large installation projects and provocative sculptures using unorthodox materials. His works are held in the permanent collections of numerous institutions, including the Metropolitan Museum of Art, the Whitney, and the Museum of Fine Arts in Houston, as well as museums in Japan, Germany, San Diego, the Bronx and Houston. Martínez Celaya contributed watercolor illustrations to *XX-Lyrics and Photographs of the Cowboy Junkies* and founded the publishing house Whale and Star. He lives and works in South Florida.

The Ultimate Challenge

– PAQUITO D'RIVERA –

I WAS A KID IN HAVANA when I had my first frontal encounter
with what Cuban percussionist Daniel Ponce used to call the "ultimate challenge"–the English language. My dad showed up at home
one day with a Benny Goodman LP recorded live at someplace
called "Carnegie Hall." Surprised, I asked, "What do you mean,
carne y frijol?" I couldn't see any possible connection between the
dish my mother cooked all the time and that exciting music played
by the Jewish clarinettist and his orchestra.

About 25 years after my father practically choked on my unin-
tentional joke, when I was out on tour with my band Irakere, I was
having breakfast in a coffee shop on Broadway. Come to think of
it, it was actually very near Carnegie Hall. While we were waiting
for our food, I heard one of the musicians from the band trying to
use English to explain to a CBS executive that he wasn't feeling
well. He said that he had eaten too much the night before and had
awakened with "*estrenyimyent.*"

"Estrenyimyent?!" the American exclaimed, trying to pronounce this strange word and wagging his head from side to side,
like a dog who doesn't understand what you're trying to teach
him. The musician was trying to say that he was having problems
voiding his bowels—in other words, that he was suffering from
estreñimiento, constipation.

As I recall, the person who produced that strange Hispanicism
from out of left field got seriously ticked off when saxophonist
Carlos Averhoff, who was also at our table, almost fell off his

seat laughing. Well, all I can say is that "Spanglish"—which has become a part of our everyday speech—is one thing, but utter nonsense is something else altogether, and it can trigger some pretty hysterical situations.

Once, when I had finally come to live in the New York City area, toward the end of 1980, one of my first jobs was substituting for José Fajardo, the famous Cuban flute player. He was so popular that he sometimes had as many as two or three *orquestas* playing at once in different parts of the city.

In those days I still lived with my mother on Overlook Terrace in West New York, New Jersey, and since Fajardo lived in our same building, he gave me a ride in his enormous station wagon one freezing Sunday to La Bilbaína restaurant on 23rd Street in Manhattan. The plan was that I would take his place in the band while he went on to Brooklyn, where he had another gig. His son Armandito, who was already playing the timbal from time to time with "Fajardo and His Stars," came along. Having been born in the United States, Armandito was perfectly bilingual and would often help his monolingual dad make himself understood.

The afternoon was clear, peaceful, and bright, and a light but chilling breeze blew over from the Hudson River, mixing with the delicious smell of Cuban cooking that emanated from Overlook Terrace. When we got out to the parking lot, people who recognized the legendary Fajardo greeted him with affection and enthusiasm. As soon as he started the engine, the radio began blaring the lively notes of "Sayonara, Sayonara, I'm Off to Japan," one of the hits that Fajardo, a country boy from Pinar del Río, had had at the end of the fifties. The radio was tuned to our neighbor Polito Vega's weekly program. Polito was a star DJ in the City.

As José, Armandito, and I started making our way up Boulevard East toward the Lincoln Tunnel, the impressive profile of the City of Skyscrapers appeared to move along the horizon as if it were alive. A group of children was placing floral offerings next to the bust of Cuban patriot José Martí on its marble pedestal in the park along the eastern sidewalk of the street.

"They say one time in a class he was teaching," I told the Fajardos, "Martí pronounced Shakespeare's name as if it were in Spanish: 'Chah-keh-SPEER-eh.' When one of the students corrected him, Martí continued the rest of the lesson in perfect English."

"Well, bro', it's a good thing I wasn't in that class, because it would've all been Greek to me, ya know?" said the elder Fajardo, with his usual country boy grin.

On the way to La Bilbaína, we stopped at a gas station to fill up the enormous wagon's gluttonous tank. "*Filirópalo, primo*!" Fajardo called out in his gravelly voice to the Pakistani station manager. It sounded like he was saying: "Feely-ROPE-alo, PREE-mo."

Protecting himself from the glacial wind that was blowing, and shivering from head to toe, the attendant pulled his wool cap down to his ears and looked at me for help. I shrugged my shoulders, and he looked over at Fajardo, who tried to clear things up.

"*Que lo filiropées, mi hermanito, 'Filiropeltan,' ¿o tú no underestán mai ingli, o qué? E'chale, primo.*"

Young Armandito read desperation in my face and came to our rescue. At that point the Pakistani and I learned that, translated from Fajardo senior's special language, he had tried to say "Fill 'er up," and that *primo*—cousin, in Spanish—had nothing to do with family relationships, but meant that he wanted the tank filled with "premium."

"Well, that's what I said, isn't it? 'Feely-ROPE-alo, PREE-mo.' Am I speaking Chinese here?!" Armandito winked at me, smiled, and after paying the confused Pakistani, we continued on our way to our matinée performance with the ineffable Fajardo and His Stars.

Another time, I was waiting for a famous American pianist to give me a ride to a gig at a jazz club in Wilmington, Delaware. At that time I was living with my folks in a neighborhood where almost everybody was either Cuban or from some other Spanish-speaking country. You hardly ever saw any Anglos in that part of Hudson County, New Jersey. (Still don't.)

"Hurry up, son! A foreigner named Tim McCoy is waiting for you," my mother told me as I was preparing for the gig.

"A foreigner named Tim McCoy, like that old cowboy in the silent movies?" I asked, mightily perplexed. "What are you talking about, Mom?"

When I got out to the living room, the "foreigner" was the great pianist McCoy Tyner, who had come to pick me up for that night's gig in Delaware.

But never mind, everybody's got their problems. I've definitely encountered my own share of stumbling blocks when it comes to the English language. Like the time I was shopping with my wife at a Korean grocery store and I asked for a "rape avocado."

The woman looked at me with disgust and answered, "You're sick."

"What?" I asked, a little frightened by the woman's tone of voice and fierce expression. Fortunately my wife spoke up, clarifying for the clerk that I was looking for a ripe avocado.

Pronunciation is an aggravating part of learning any language, especially when you find words that to the ear of a Spanish speaker sound a lot like each other. For example, I prefer to say that I'm going "to the seashore" or "to the ocean," because "beach" is something completely different from "bitch." If I get it wrong and say "I'm going to the bitch," I'll sound like I'm going out for a wild night with prostitutes.

Another example is "sheet," as in sheets for a bed or a sheet of paper, as opposed to "shit." That's why, in my profession, I always refer to "piano parts," because if I say "lead sheet" and it comes out "lead shit," God knows what kind of reaction I might get from American musicians.

Saying in English "Aunt Ann and an Ant," just sounds to us like someone trying to talk with his nose stuffed up. And you can imagine what a challenge it is to understand a language in which "ass" means "donkey," but also "butt." How the heck do you say "the ass's ass"?

I am convinced that the most challenging part of a language is not speaking it, but understanding it, especially since, to make things even more complicated, there's the whole accent thing. One of my first experiences with strange accents was at the beginning of one of my first on-stage appearances with Dizzy Gillespie, the trumpet player who was a huge help in getting my career into high gear in the competitive world of jazz.

Dizzy was born in Cheraw, South Carolina, and we all know what those Southern accents are like, don't we? Well, it was the opening night of Rockhead's Paradise, the famous Montreal jazz club. We were already on stage when I asked Dizzy what we were going to play. He answered with a noise that sounded like something between the underwater braying of a Cambodian buffalo and the snoring sound made by a diesel motor with carburetor problems.

I swallowed and asked Ed Cherry, the guitarist, who was next to me, "What did Gillespie say?"

"How the heck should I know?" he answered simply.

"What do you mean you don't know?! You're American, aren't you?"

"Yes, but he's from South Carolina, and that's another planet, bro'. Better wait 'til he starts to play, and you'll know right away where the shots are coming from."

He was right. And I learned once more that music, and especially jazz, is the true universal language, the language of love, tolerance, and respect for free expression that flows between those who speak it and their audiences.

On the other hand, there is no doubt that, precisely due to its simplicity and practicality, the language of Shakespeare (or "Chah-keh-SPEER-eh," as Martí liked to say) has become what people tried to create through Esperanto many years ago. That is to say, it has become a language that people of different latitudes can use to facilitate better communication amongst themselves. On top of that—and despite the extreme difficulty some people may have understanding English—if we look at the subject with objectivity and optimism, you'd have to admit that things could have been a lot worse if we had had to break the frustrations of the language barrier in Cantonese, Urdu, or Bulgarian, don't you agree?

Winner of numerous Grammy awards, clarinet and saxophone virtuoso **PAQUITO D'RIVERA** (Havana, Cuba; 1948-) began his performing career with Cuba's Orquesta Sinfónica Nacional and later was cofounder of the explosive fusion group Irakere. His accolades include the Annual Achievement in Music Award from the National Hispanic Academy of Media Arts and Sciences and designation as a Jazz Master by the National Endowment for the Arts. He is artist in residence at the New Jersey Performing Arts Center and the author of *My Sax Life: A Memoir*. In 2007 he was awarded a Guggenheim Fellowship.

The Mexicans Who Speak English

– ANONYMOUS –

Excerpted from *A Texas-Mexican Cancionero: Folksongs of the Lower Border.*

In Texas it is terrible how things are all mixed up;
no one says "hasta mañana," it's nothing but "goodbye."

And "howdy-dee-do, my friend, and I'll see you tomorrow";
when they want to say "diez reales" they say "dollar and a quarter."

I made love to a Texas-Mexican girl, one of those with a parasol;
I said to her, "Will you go along with me?" and she told me,
"Looky heah!"

I made love to another fashionable lady, one of those with a garsolé;
I said to her, "Will you go along with me?" and she told me, "What
you say?"

Then I went to the depot to talk to Doña Inés;
I talked to her in Spanish, and she answered me in English.

All of us want to speak the American language,
without understanding our own Spanish tongue.

In Texas it is terrible how things are all mixed up;
no one says "hasta mañana," it's nothing but "goodbye."

AMÉRICO PAREDES (Brownsville, Texas; 1915-1999), compiler of *A Texas-Mexican Cancionero: Folksongs of the Lower Border*, received his doctorate in English and folklore, subjects that dominated his long career at the University of Texas. He received major prizes from both the U.S. and Mexican governments for his studies of borderland culture. Credited with according academic rigor and respect to border songs, humor, and oral tradition, Paredes is the author of the classic study, *"With His Pistol in His Hand": A Border Ballad and Its Hero*.

Dangerous English

— JOHANNA CASTILLO —

WHEN I THINK ABOUT learning English, I instantly remember the old English-language movies and records I owned as a kid. I grew up in Guayaquil, Ecuador, where the main language is Spanish, but for some reason I was fascinated by English. When I was six, I would dance and sing for hours to the music of *Grease*. I was a big fan of John Travolta and Olivia Newton-John and learned all of their songs before moving on to my two older sisters' Madonna and Cindy Lauper records.

As my attraction to the English language grew, I would stand in front of the mirror practicing new song lyrics and their pronunciation. My friends and I would pretend that we were speaking English when it was really just gibberish. My father used to say, "M'ija, the only way to learn a new language is to read the dictionary."

I was an avid reader by the age of 12 and, oddly, I mostly read Spanish translations of American classics, from Hemingway to Whitman. I don't know why I chose those books. Maybe I had foreseen my future life in the United States.

My interest in English continued to grow, and my parents sent me to a bilingual school for the last three years of high school. Each day was taught half in English and half in Spanish. The classes in English included history of the United States, grammar, conversation, and geography. Most of my classmates were perfectly bilingual. I certainly wasn't, but somehow I survived and graduated with good grades.

At 17 I began my career in finance and banking at the Universidad Espíritu Santo in Guayaquil. I also got my first job at Banco del Progreso, one of the most prestigious banks in Ecuador. Even though I was moving up the corporate ladder at a very young age, I always felt that not knowing English was keeping me from a world full of new opportunities. The university that I was attending had an exchange program with the State University of New York at New Paltz. The program had only two openings each year. I decided to apply and at the same time take intensive English classes. The most difficult requirement was the interview—in English, of course—with the director of the program. I hired a tutor and took classes daily for months. Finally, I won a spot to study in the States, and five months later I arrived in New Paltz, New York. After realizing that nobody spoke Spanish in this small town, I was on the fast track to learning English. Just imagine a woman unable to talk!

My experience at SUNY New Paltz was wonderful. I had classmates from all over the world: Spain, Greece, China, Japan, Brazil, and other nations. I took grammar, history, lab classes, and my favorite, "Dangerous English." In this class we learned about U.S. culture and how different actions or words can be misunderstood. For example, we were taught that when you have a conversation with an American, you need to keep one arm's distance from that person. (In Latin America we talk very close to each other.) Also, that when you meet someone in an informal situation, you first offer your hand, never a kiss on the cheek. (We kiss everyone on the cheek in Latin America—except in a business environment.) That's still difficult for me to adapt to after all these years, so now I usually offer my hand and then I offer a kiss on the cheek.

Since coming here, I have been in love with this wonderful language. It will be forever a part of my life and a reminder that we can learn something new—even if just a new word—every day.

JOHANNA CASTILLO (Guayaquil, Ecuador; 1975-) works as a senior editor at a major New York publishing house. Prior to her current position she represented Latino authors as an agent at the Sanford Greenburger Literary Agency.

Ay Doan Peek Eenglee
or
No me pica la ingle
(My Groin Doesn't Itch)

— JOSÉ KOZER —

AS A KID I USED TO SIT on the red tiles of the terrace of our house in Havana and start speaking languages. I got to be pretty good at it, inventing 14 of them. One of them was English. As a language it seemed less interesting to me than, say, Chinese or Urdu, the latter being a language of which I had complete command by the age of ten.

I must have taken English for years, in elementary as well as secondary school. The secondary school course of study is called *bachillerato* in Spanish, but we used to call it bachiverraco, *verraco* meaning "swine." It was an apt designation when you understand that we emerged from years of study speaking with the vocabulary of an injured mule. From all that study of English, I remember hardly more than a few phrases, a word here and there (nothing more complicated than "Tom is a boy," "Mary is a girl"). Nor do I remember what textbook we used, what poems they made us memorize in English, or what idioms we could rely on knowing when it came time to put into practice what we had learned—or rather not learned.

Of that experience, lasting years, I remember nothing. I do, however, have a vague recollection of an English teacher I had in the last few years of secondary school, whom we all liked (especially the girls): tall, blond, ungainly, always cheerful, I remember that he spoke Spanish fluently, but with a certain strange inflection, and that he would sometimes put his foot in his mouth by mixing up the word *inglés* (English) with *ingle* (groin). I do know that he was one of the first to jump ship when the revolution came. And I understand that in Miami he started a store selling *shmattes*, which made it possible for him to lead a life of leisure. I was happy to hear that. I think that a teacher who ended up selling rags for a living was probably a shoddy teacher and, after years of going around in circles, simply found his true vocation.

Upon my arrival in New York in 1960 at age 20, I estimate that my English vocabulary consisted of "dog," "why not?" and "of course." Aside from that scanty knowledge, the remnant of my decade-long study of the English language in one of Cuba's best schools, I don't believe I was able to say anything, but rather got what I needed by pointing or making Cuban-style gestures: cigarettes, a package of sugar, my first job.

What miracle made it possible for me, three months after my arrival in New York, to be working as sales manager of an import-export company on Wall Street? I can't explain it. Maybe the bosses took a liking to me. Maybe the faltering steps of my first babbling attempts in English amused them. Maybe they realized that this particular immigrant would be easy to exploit. Whatever the case, I was there for three years, managing the commercial operations of that small corporation. I sold light airplanes, autopilots, King radios, and replacement parts for single-engine planes.

And all in English. I wrote business letters with the dictionary lying open on the work table, letters that became so formulaic that after the first two weeks I hardly needed the book anymore. I learned that minimal amount of English necessary to swindle one's neighbor, to buy cheap and sell at three times the price, or to convince someone to buy a small plane—either for use in one's own country to earn money (swindling, in turn, one's fellow countrymen) or, alternatively, to buy it for personal use, becoming indebted for life.

After the third year of working there, I took off. And I took off in English, to start a career in the literature of the Spanish and Portuguese languages at New York University (which, pronounced Cuban-style, "En Guay Yu," certainly resembles Chinese more than English).

Now, I halfway knew business English, as well as the English I was picking up on the streets and in the alleyways of Greenwich Village. At the same time, I was starting to read T. S. Eliot, Wallace Stevens, and William Carlos Williams with a certain level of agility. My knowledge of English was growing: the streets, bohemian life, alcohol, some randomly encountered fight, the perpetual lack of money that gave me an excuse to let my hair grow long—all these circumstances gave me a basic, oral English. Though it was rarely written by me, it was good enough to get a 50-dollar-a-week-plus-tuition job as a gofer in the university's Science Library. If there was a problem, it was that, given my Cuban accent, I was always obliged to avoid the dangers of using certain words that were impossible to pronounce in English, such as "beach," which to me sounded exactly like "bitch"; "sheet," which to me was a homonym with "shit"; or "peace," which emerged from my mouth with the same sound I made when saying "piss." I got used to substituting: instead of "beach," I would say "shore"; instead of "sheet," "a piece of paper" or "linen"; and instead of "peace," something like "One should always avoid war."

Somewhere around 1965—married to an American woman, studying mostly in English, speaking and reading English all day—I noticed something happening to me: I was losing my native language at an accelerated rate. At the same time, my new language wasn't really taking off or even growing within me. And since I have had the need to write poetry since I was 15 years old, I suddenly realized that I was lacking the very tool that makes poetic writing possible: a mother tongue.

I went ten years without being able to write a single poem. I would start them and pretty soon they would abort on me, due to a lack of language. And it wasn't a question of using or not using a dictionary, but rather a lack of natural contact with my own language. I lived exclusively in an English that I continued to learn in the verbal fights I had with my first wife in the bars of the Village (there was no expletive I did not learn), and in the formal, tedious classes of the university. I still remember the comments of one English professor handing back one of my compositions on the picaresque novel, full of red ink blots: "Your ideas are very good, but you don't know how to write English." When his back was turned, I launched an "I just got off the banana boat, what do you want from me?" attack.

I called the only complete poem that I wrote during that time "Go South Travel Greyhound." It was written in my burlesque, imitative Spanish of that period. It was completely impossible for me to write poetry in Spanish and even less in English, a language that I did not feel, either superficially or deep within. It was a language that I did not need, given that what I needed was to write poetry. And I could only do that in the language I had suckled from the breast: Spanish—a Spanish that had vanished.

Vanished, but slowly reappeared, little by little. Around 1970 the language that had been lost—or rather bottled up in my psychic system—manifested itself once again. From that time on, my English remained in place, more or less static, while my relationship with Spanish grew stronger, proliferative, plural, and ecumenical. Thus, I can say that I learned English by resisting it. I learned it and studied it, while also evading it enough so that my Spanish, natural and unruly, did not weaken, but rather matured in all its multifaceted forms in Spain and Latin America.

English is a language that I love. Deeply. I read it with satisfaction and pleasure, and for me it is a true privilege to have this tool at my disposal to penetrate the depths of Joyce, Faulkner, or Zukofsky; Charles Olson, Guy Davenport, or Henry James. But it is a language that I must resist in order to continue writing poetry, poetry which I can create only in my mother tongue. My Spanish was decomposed and recomposed through the experience of exile, the diaspora of the word. English is one of the two languages I use in daily life, one of my two greatest treasures, but I must keep it at bay. Otherwise it would keep me from maintaining the degree of poems that I have been sustaining for decades.

In my old age I don't feel threatened by English. Lately I have even been giving myself the luxury of dreaming in English. Likewise, I read vociferously every day, alternating a book in Spanish with one in English. I sometimes ask myself whether I will die in Spanish or in English.

JOSÉ KOZER (Havana, Cuba; 1940-) has written more than 50 books and chapbooks of poetry published in Spain, the United States, and seven Latin American nations. His most recent book is *Stet,* which presents his career's work bilingually. He lives near Miami.

Amerika, America

− ILAN STAVANS −

Excerpted from *On Borrowed Words* {*A Memoir of Language*}

I INVOKE MOBY-DICK. Who could have told me I would one day learn English–my English–thanks to it? I flew across the Rio Grande with very primitive language skills, but one night, in my small bedroom at Broadway and 122nd Street, I made a commitment to myself: America had opened its arms to me, having proffered a full fellowship to perform graduate studies; in return, I should turn it into my America, I would attempt to perfect my English as much as I could and become a useful citizen. In my practical mind, the term "useful" carried a concrete meaning: a voice to count, to listen to. I was in my mid-20s, more than capable of self-knowledge. After all, I had taught myself to appreciate Jewishness anew in Ciudad de México, and in Israel I forced myself to read Tchernichowsky and Bialik in the original. Why couldn't I vastly improve my skills in the tongue of Shakespeare, make myself literally fluent in it, as fluent, as Joseph Conrad would say, "as an unimpeded river"?

Those were nights of verbal definition–lonely nights, enraptured by the music of words. To make ends meet, aside from my duties as a correspondent for Mexican newspapers and my studies, I also worked at the translation agency of Columbia University. Once or twice a week, the agency would send me a set of legal documents or a short story or would ask me to meet such-and-such a person to teach him or her an hour's worth of Spanish. These efforts were an invaluable exercise to me; indeed, I'm still amazed today at my fearlessness, for the requests were always to render a text into English, in which I was weak, and hardly ever the other way around. But it was in *Moby-Dick* that I found my true teacher. The method was simple yet dogmatic: with my atrocious pronunciation, I would read a single paragraph, sometimes even a single line, at low speed: "Kol mi Ismael. Som yiars agou—never maind jau long precaiseli —jabin litel or no moni in mai purz, and nottin parhkular tu interes mi on shour, ai tout ai bud seil abaut a litel and si de guatery part of de gorld." With a pad in hand, I would make a list of all the words I had failed to understand, without looking for a definition in my pocket-size *Oxford English Dictionary*, which my father had given to me as a present; I would then put the book aside, turn the light off, and repeat the list in order. At this time came the best part of all: I would try to imagine what these words meant. I would then turn the light on again, look in the dictionary for the right response, smiling at how off target I had been, and finish by going over the list again, this time repeating to myself what each word really meant. The following night, I would read the segment again and repeat the list from memory. Obviously, this was a nightmarish approach; it taught me much but eliminated all possible pleasure from the act of reading itself.

English is almost mathematical. Its rules manifest themselves in an iron fashion. This is in sharp contrast to Spanish, of course, whose Romance roots make it a free-flowing, imprecise language, with long and uncooperative words. As a language, it is somewhat undeserving of the literature it has created. This might explain why I enjoy rereading *One Hundred Years of Solitude* far more in English than in the original, as well as *Don Quixote*. For me, mastering English was, as I convinced myself, a ticket to salvation. Spanish, in spite of being the third most important language on the globe, after Chinese and English, is peripheral. It is a language that flourishes in the outskirts of culture, more reactive than active.

The immediate results of my reading methods were less than gratifying. The response I got to the dispatches I sent to the newspapers *Excelsior* and *La Jornada* was univocal: I was writing in Spanish, editors would claim, but thinking in English; my grammar was bizarre, polluted, unconvincing. They often sent the wired articles back with endless nasty comments. This tension achieved its climax when, in a trip to Mexico, I stopped by the offices of *Unomásuno*, one of the newspapers I occasionally wrote for, and Humberto Batis, a ruffian of a veteran, told me to stop writing altogether. "Your future, my friend, might as well be in business!"

ILAN STAVANS (Mexico City, Mexico; 1961-) has written more than a dozen books and served as editor of as many more. Among his own titles are *On Borrowed Words: A Memoir of Language* and *The One-Handed Pianist, and Other Stories*. His anthologies include *The Poetry of Pablo Neruda* and *The Oxford Book of Latin American Essays*. Stavans, who hosted a PBS interview show in Boston for five years called *La Plaza*, is the Lewis-Sebring Professor in Latin American and Latino Culture at Amherst College in Massachusetts.

José Manué...
You Don't Know
No English

— JESÚS VEGA —

IN THE SIXTIES, the Cuban education system adopted a new tool that, though it would experience the same fate as all the other failed revolutionary inventions, at least was popular among the students at the time: Soviet televisions filled the middle and high school classrooms so students could watch math, chemistry, and English classes taught by smiling professors who blinked continually, blinded by the lights of the studio.

The classes were offered at midday, and on many occasions served as a sleeping tonic for the students, who generally arrived drowsy after walking beneath the Caribbean sun or after hanging from the doors of overstuffed noontime buses. The snoring droned on especially during the math sessions, a constant background beneath the monotone voice of the professors on the screen. But the sleepiness dissipated once the next session began: the English class, which always began with an instrumental version of "And I Love Her" by Santo & Johnny. These sessions offered a glimpse into that fascinating language that could be heard, like a message of promise, in the broadcasts of the radio stations, especially WQAM (*la Dóbliu*) from Miami and KAAY (*Keieieiuai*) from Little Rock. These stations had thousands of followers on the Havana beaches and streets alike. Prohibited fruit, generator of music officially condemned as an "ideological diversion."

Studying English brought us closer to those distant echoes, as they carried visions of a different and unknown world from across the sea. For this reason, even the most morose student concentrated in those classes, which were later complemented by a session with a live instructor. Everyone took notes zealously, and the homework and individual projects were never neglected from the scarce study materials, each student working with feverish enthusiasm.

The English professors also enjoyed an aura of respect from the students. Many were "repatriates" who had returned from the United States at the beginning of the revolution, while others were communists or fugitives from justice who had sought refuge on Fidel's island. Thanks to these instructors, who pushed to impart greater knowledge than the limited curriculum imposed, we escaped the tedium and moved closer, although at a turtle's pace, to conquering what was now being called the "language of the enemy."

For me, these classes were the culmination of a fascination begun in childhood. My grandmother had told me of American marines disembarking in Matanzas, and Cuban boys (who were not allowed to smoke) learning to ask them for cigarettes by saying *yimi un sigarét*. That phrase held a certain exotic significance for me and inspired me to search for any related word, particularly in the animated cartoons of *Gato Félix* (*Felix the Cat*), *La pequeña Lulú* (*Little Lulu*), and *Tom y Jerry*, and in the episodes of *Bat Masterson*, *Patrulla de Caminos* (*Highway Patrol*), or *El Llanero Solitario* (*The Lone Ranger*), where, despite the Spanish voice-over, you could still hear a protagonist's name or two, or read the signs announcing Saloon, Police, or Railroad.

Sadly, those programs disappeared from television, and I had to wait some years before studying English again, this time in junior high. The programs were also the answer to many questions, and the reason for which, on one occasion, I ran into a big problem in elementary school when I told my classmates my father worked for the Sía. Immediately I was marched to the office, where a teacher submitted me to extensive questioning. They left me in the office until it was time to go home, when my mother appeared to assure them that the proclaimed Sía was not the dreaded CIA, but the Sears branch office on the corner of Amistad and Reina.

My desire to learn awakened the sympathy of Rosalina Brown, a repatriated professor of respectable age. We called her "Tábata Tuichi," a name inspired by the protagonist of a popular song of the time, the Spanish version of "Tabatha Twitchit," the well-known piece immortalized by the Dave Clark Five. "La tícher Tuichi" was quite witty, and she killed us with her jokes, ingenious phrases, mnemonic devices, and words of advice taken from real life that always made us think. One of her unforgettable techniques involved comparing and using fragments of Beatles songs to aid comprehension, such as "If any time you feel a pain," and "If any time you fill a pen." And if someone complained or had difficulty pronouncing a word she had covered over and over, she gave a friendly laugh and urged us to keep trying with a phrase from the poetry of Nicolás Guillén: "José Manué… Tú no sabe inglé" (José Manué, you don't know no English").

"Tábata" sympathized with me, and halfway through junior high she began loaning me some old copies of magazines like *Punch*, then a pocket novel or two, never longer than 50 pages, but that nonetheless took me nearly a week to read. When I occasionally became frustrated by the difficulty of certain words, I fell behind and built up a sizable backlog of reading material.

Our friendship was strengthened even more when I found her one Sunday in church. There, in assured privacy, and in English, she confessed to me in a conspiratorial tone her frustration with what was happening in the country, her regrets at having returned as a "repatriate" and her ideas of returning to the United States, a reverse emigration. A few weeks later, she disappeared from school and we got a substitute professor we teasingly called *El Farallón* ("The Hulk") for his sheer size. Farallón was not a repatriate, nor did he know any English, so we changed his name to "José Manué."

Months later, after Mass one Sunday, one of the nuns at the church handed me a packet wrapped in newspaper and carefully tied. Upon opening it and seeing its contents, I realized that Tábata had left without saying goodbye. Later I learned that the school administrators, once they learned her plans, had fired her. But "la tícher," like a phoenix, had resisted to the very end by giving private classes.

Among the books she had left me was an old Webster's dictionary, a collection of poems by Robert Frost, and a pocket thesaurus that, scribbled in the first page, had the name of a long-forgotten previous owner: Guillermo Cabrera Infante.

The following year, the Soviet television sets began to fall apart, and our English classes lost their luster in competition with the Russian language. Russian began to be taught in a more populist dimension, via radio, in courses that never reached anyone.

Poet and critic **JESÚS VEGA** (Havana, Cuba; 1954-) works as a translator for a number of outlets and is the author of the short-story collection *Wunderbahr, maravilloso* and the film book *El cartel de cine cubano,* as well as *Zavattini en La Habana.* He has translated Julia Alvarez's *Saving the World* and *Player's Vendetta: A Little Havana Mystery,* by John Lantigua, into Spanish.

The Tremendous Assimilation Happened to Me

— PIRI THOMAS —

Excerpted from *Conversations with Ilan Stavans*

I REMEMBER WITH ALL MY heart and soul the first words I learned from Mami and Papi were all in Spanish, but as I grew up I knew that I was not speaking Spanish from Galicia or Barcelona in Spain. I was speaking the Spanish that is spoken in Puerto Rico, which I call Puerto Rican Spanish, because we kept our nuances and feeling and energies and words that came from Africa, like *chévere*, which means great. We are a mixture of all those who conquered us over the centuries, taking our women with or without permission. We are a culmination of all that energy, but our spirit is as free as it was born to be. We are a conglomeration of manifestations...

I began to go though the same process as everyone has undergone under the system, beginning with the Native Americans: the assimilation process. I remember in my own childhood in the thirties being in this school and I could not understand what the teacher was saying so much, because they spoke fast sometimes and I could not catch the words. I'd lean over to my friend, saying "José, mira, what did the teacher say?" He would tell me and I would continue to do my homework. And so that teacher came roaring upon me and said, "Listen, stop talking in that language." And I said, "Well, I'm speaking my mother's language. My mother's from Puerto Rico; I was born in this country." And she says, "You stop talking that, you have to learn English, you are in America now.

After all, how else do you expect to become president of the United States if you do not learn to speak English correctly?" I thought in my young heart, "My God, this teacher has more faith than I have in my someday becoming president of the United States if I learn English well enough." And the tremendous assimilation happened to me. As a child, I first had to think in Spanish to speak in English. Then, I had to think in English to speak in Spanish, because I had forgotten the language. I had forgotten the lessons that were taught in my home.

PIRI THOMAS (New York, New York; 1928-) was born in Spanish Harlem. He served time for armed robbery as a youth, a sentence that led to his autobiographical *Down These Mean Streets*. It was followed by *Savior, Savior Hold My Hand*, *Seven Long Times*, and *Stories from El Barrio*. He has been profiled in three films, including *Every Child Is Born a Poet: The Life and Work of Piri Thomas*, was a member of the Harlem Writers Guild, and recently was awarded the PEN New England Thomas Paine Freedom to Write award.

Once Upon a Time on the Border

— GABRIEL TRUJILLO MUÑOZ —

WHEN I WAS A CHILD of no more than five years, having barely begun to decipher the world and its alphabet, I paged through the enormous book that occupied the place of pride on the family shelf: the Holy Bible, published in 1961 with the blessing of Pope Pius XII. But I found it more terrifying than marvelous because of its engravings by Augusto Doré, whose realism made me shudder. The engraving which made the deepest impression on me was the Tower of Babel. My mother explained that the punishment for the sheer arrogance of trying to build it was that the builders were made to speak a variety of languages, which kept them from going on, since they no longer understood each other. That explanation gave rise to my first metaphysical doubt: if the people spoke different languages, different tongues, then why was Mexicali, the Mexican border town where I was born in 1958, a metropolis that prospered, in defiance of biblical punishment? And that is how, in that city which bordered the United States of America, I realized we were an anomaly, a world apart.

In Mexicali it was easy to learn that the more varied the inhabitants, the more we worked for the common good: just surviving in the desert, with its summer temperatures higher than 100 degrees in the shade, as a community made up of Mexicans from every corner of the country and the foreigners who lived alongside us, all striving to make an agricultural village into a proper city. Around the corner from my house was a grocery store that belonged to an

old Chinese man who could barely ask, "What do you want?–
¿qué quelel tú?" and spent all day reading newspapers in Cantonese.
Down the block was a Japanese notions shop where they sold
Godzilla toys and sheets of rice paper, and then there were families
whose children were in the army or navy, who spoke only Spanish
with their parents, and campers with retired people from the United
States, the so-called snowbirds who had decided to end their lives
in a Mexican refuge where it was warm and cheap, sitting in nylon
chairs and singing Irish songs of war and lost love. It was the whole
world in one neighborhood. I could hear polkas and mariachis,
Japanese and Peking opera all at the same time. It was a triumphant
Babel, defying divine punishment by proving that diversity is better
than uniformity.

It was there in my childhood home, only five blocks from the international border, that I decided language would not prevent me from
knowing others, and through them–my neighbors, my kinsmen–
knowing myself. That was before I went to school where English was
a basic subject and I learned my first words in another language.

My parents had been married in the south of the country and
were recent arrivals. My father, Gabriel Trujillo Chacón, a radio
operator with the Mexican Aviation Company at the Mexicali airport, spoke English with the pilots who flew along the border, and
my mother, Margarita Muñoz López, was an enterprising housewife and capable manager of my progenitor's salary. I was an only
child, and on weekends we went to the nearby California cities of
Calexico and El Centro with two goals in mind: to shop and to
eat at a restaurant buffet. Shopping meant asking the salesperson
the price of each can or item. "How much?" was the crucial question and soon I, a child who wanted everything I saw, heard those
magical words and believed they meant, "Give me that now." And
since the salespeople were solicitous and handed me boxes with
fire trucks, pistols that fired corks, or astronaut suits, I believed
them mine forever, or at least until I destroyed them by too much

hard play. My parents then had to remove those shining marvels and return them to their places. So I learned something else, which I thought must mean, "We'll come back later for your gift," as they hastened to tell the salespeople, "I'm sorry, not now." And just when I was about to burst into tears, they gave me a can of spinach with a picture of Popeye the Sailor, so I'd forget my troubles. Then we'd go to Cameo, a restaurant decorated with photos of cowboys herding livestock, and horseshoes in every corner. My parents called the waitresses "Miss" and I learned that word, too.

I entered Catholic elementary school knowing the English word, "Miss." At school all our teachers were religious and wore rigorous vestments and the look of ill-tempered jailers, all but Señorita Lupita, the English teacher, a young woman of the mid-1970s, whose skirts crept above her knees and whose blouses revealed her secret curves. On the first day, Lupita asked us to call her "Miss" and we all recited in chorus:

"Good morning, Miss."

Miss replied, "Good morning, children."

If I thought I'd learn English in class, I didn't; I only learned to gaze at Miss in a trance. One hour every day lost in daydreams. Of course, I acquired a few rote expressions: "Hello, friends," "What day is today?" "I'm a boy and I am seven years old," "I live in Mexicali and Mexico is my country," and "I want to be an airline pilot." But I soon discovered that English was offered everywhere, even at recess. I must have been eight or nine years old when we got together on the soccer field to eat lunch. The conversation drifted through the television programs dubbed in Spanish, from *Los locos Addams* (*The Addams Family*) to *La dimensión desconocid* (*The Twilight Zone*) to *La ley del revolve* (*Have Gun, Will Travel*). As we grew older, the talk turned to music, to the groups we all followed with hypnotic enthusiasm. We fought between Beatles fans and Rolling Stones fans.

At home, my parents listened to *rancheras*, Cuban *boleros*, and Argentine tangos; sad songs of lost love. But the English music was pure energy—vibrating rhythm, shouts and cries, explosive melodies that left us no peace. And later we learned the words. At recess we would sing "She Loves You" or "Ruby Tuesday" as if we were Lennon or Jagger, everyone repeating the chorus, "Yeah, yeah, yeah!"

The nuns thought we were lost causes and prayed for us. I saw I would have to learn English to understand the words. I didn't want to be "The Fool on the Hill," I wanted to be "Jumping Jack Flash" or to meet "Lucy in the Sky with Diamonds." I began to see that English opened the door to a culture full of wild imagination and fantasies that complemented my own. But my mother always told me the most important English words, the ones I should never forget, were "Thank you."

I was grateful that movies in English had subtitles instead of being dubbed. To hear the language of Shakespeare while reading a translation into Castellano was something that, even to this day, taught me a sense of humor. So when someone makes me crazy, I put on my Clint Eastwood face and tell them, "Come on, make my day," or when someone serves me a meal I detest, I put on Marlon Brando and mutter, "The horror, the horror," or when I see what a mess the world is in, I think about *Casablanca* and say to myself, "You must remember this / A kiss is just a kiss / A sigh is just a sigh…."

In middle school, as in elementary school, I was an average student. A teenage male with asthma, sedentary, who spent a lot of time reading and writing under the spell of Jules Verne, Emilio Salgari, Ray Bradbury, Pablo Neruda, and Alexandre Dumas. I realized I was advancing in my ability to read and write English, but that I fell short in speaking. Certainly I had opportunities to practice my stammering English on the other side on the border. But living in Mexicali, a city of more than 400,000 souls facing Calexico, which didn't have a tenth of our population, whenever I asked for something in English, the salespeople answered in Spanish, so I had no need for English to communicate.

My father attended my graduation from prep school in June 1975. A few days later I went to Guadalajara, in the interior of the country, to study medicine. There, 1,300 miles from the border, I found out how lucky I was to be able to read the medical texts in English, because the Spanish editions only came out some five years later. And those five years meant an unacceptable delay in learning the latest surgical techniques or laboratory tests, therapies, or medicines to employ against the multitude of illnesses that attacked humanity.

English helped me be up to date and not held back in the arts and sciences that interested me. But my university companions believed that my stammering meant I was a *pocho*, *agringado*, Americanized. It was a popular prejudice: English was not something we Mexicans should know, and learning it made us less Mexican. I, on the other hand, assured them that to know another culture through a language made me more interested in my own culture and I wanted to show it to the whole world. *The best of two worlds.*

Six years later, in 1981, I returned to Mexicali with my medical degree—specialties in surgery and childbirth—under my arm. During the 1980s I had a private medical practice, but I also took up creative writing and teaching at the Autonomous University of Baja California. I eventually stopped practicing medicine entirely and dedicated myself full-time to literature and academics. But I needed a piece of paper to prove I spoke English. I decided to study English at San Diego State University's Imperial Valley campus. There I met Alurista, the Chicano poet who became famous for bringing the myth of Aztlán to the Chicano movement in the form of a poem.

"Why are you so interested in English?" asked Alurista.

"Because it allows me to see the United States as a dialogue and not a confrontation. There are so many voices, so many truths in every word, in every sentence. English helps me value my own language, Spanish, and offers me a smorgasbord of ideas and visions where I take what I need and like. English allows me to see the world as a current that changes at every moment and not as something fixed and eternal. It gives me choices in rhythm, tone, and discernment."

And that's how it's been ever since.

Today English is open to other languages, and so is Spanish. To live on the border means being the vanguard of a movement that is global and democratic, capable of taking in both its own and the Other, native and foreign, strengthening ourselves as a culture and adapting to the changing world, living our lives with real opportunities for creativity and persistance, will and work, art and passion. A window that is always open, where my house is your house, my Spanish is your English, and my culture is your culture. In any case, to learn another language is to lose the fear of the others who are our neighbors, and to see the United States neither as ogre nor paradise but as a country like our own, with its own problems and conflicts. English is a bridge—never a wall—that communicates and connects us.

I must admit, in this 21st century, that I am still learning English at almost 50 years old. While I look for books and records at the Borders in San Diego or listen to the music of Franz Ferdinand and Depeche Mode at the Coachella Music Festival, or watch the excellent adventures of *Buffy the Vampire Slayer,* I know that for me, English opened the doors of perception to other worlds as valuable and imaginative as our own. While I read the novels of Michael Connelly and Paco Ignacio Taibo II or listen to the music of Mecano and Patti Smith, I know that English and Spanish are steps toward the Babel of our times: a project we do together, a tower built with the promise of better understanding among all of us.

At my side, my girlfriend Karla shows me a disc of the Flaming Lips.

"Is this what you were looking for?"

I agree with a wide grin. And I can only sing, like the child I am: "Yeah, yeah, yeah!"

And so on a voyage through language, like a journey with no return, if anyone asks me when I learned English, I simply reply, "I'm learning it now and forever."

GABRIEL TRUJILLO MUÑOZ (Mexicali, Mexico; 1958-), a professor at the Universidad Autónoma de Baja California in Mexicali, is the author of *Mercaderes*, a short-story collection; *Rastrojo*, selected poetry; *Lengua Franca*, a book of essays; and numerous other titles. Trujillo, also the compiler of the *Bibliographic Dictionary of Baja California Writers*, was awarded the binational Pellicer-Frost poetry prize in 1996.

Better English through Unions

— BYRON SILVA —

I SPOKE NO ENGLISH my first seven years in the United States. For most of that time, until the year 2000, I often had to juggle three jobs to keep up with the bills. Mainly I worked in the asbestos industry, but I also worked in a bakery and in retail sales. In each environment I spoke 100 percent Spanish. In all that time, it was Spanish television, Spanish radio, Spanish supervisors. I felt no need to learn English.

I didn't know it at the time, but the Laborers International Union of North America (LIUNA) had launched an organizing campaign for asbestos workers in 1996. I didn't even know that such a thing as unions existed in the United States. Three years later, while I was on a job at Montefiore Hospital in the Bronx, my coworkers and I were herded into a basement and told to keep quiet. I didn't know what was going on. I found out we were put there to avoid contact with a LIUNA representative. When the same agent showed up the next day at lunchtime, he sat down and we talked, in Spanish, of course. He explained to me that "union" was the same as "*sindicato*" in Ecuador, my native land. We began a conversation that dramatically changed my life. I joined LIUNA right away.

Even when I became shop steward with LIUNA, the union population I worked with was almost completely Spanish-speaking, and the training sessions were always bilingual. I could be useful to the union because the nonunion workforce is mostly Spanish-speaking as well. But when I joined the Laborers' Eastern Region Organizing Fund (LEROF) in 2000, there was a lot of training, and most of the meetings were in English. I was lost. I would sit and take notes, writing out words phonetically, then bringing them home to my cousin who would try to help me translate my notes into Spanish.

In Spanish, you spell words pretty much the way they sound, but it's not so easy with English. My cousin was the one who got me into the asbestos industry, but he had an accident and while he was on disability he went to Baruch College and learned English very well. Those first few months at LEROF were tough. My supervisor helped me learn the construction industry and also English. I picked up elementary grammar guides. I listened to 1010 WINS all-news radio. I read magazines and books.

I was sent to a number of pretty serious training sessions dealing with the history of the labor movement and the development of LEROF. I mean, history is difficult as it is, even in your native language. There was a lot of homework and papers to write, which was twice as much work for me since I had to translate everything before I could study it. I studied LEROF union history almost every night and on weekends. I got one of those electronic translators, which was very helpful. The first year on that job was tough, but little by little, this new language started making sense to me. Now, a few years later, I can think in both languages, and it's thrilling not to have to go back and forth in my head all the time.

From the moment I joined the union, my life had completely changed. I had decent benefits for the first time, so my family could go to a doctor and not spend a lot of money. Most important, I was able to help others who were in a situation like the one I had been in. I could make them aware of their rights and teach them how to take advantage of them. Some contractors out there are responsible and look out for the safety of their workers, but a lot of them just don't care. They'll risk the lives of the workers just to make a bigger profit.

In the department where I work at LEROF, there are six or seven different languages spoken. We see a lot of immigrants in construction—

Brazilians and Portuguese, but also Albanians, Yugoslavians, you name it. The goal is to have a staff that can talk to all nonunion workers from different backgrounds and cultures so we can help them improve their conditions and maybe move out of the construction industry. One time on Long Island, I went to talk to a crew that was all Mexican. They were very nice, very polite and all, but I knew I wasn't really welcome. We weren't able to really communicate with them until I came back with a Mexican coworker.

Right now I'm researching the hazardous waste management industry, including the cleanup in the World Trade Center after 9/11. There are many unexplained illnesses, and even deaths. We are filing Freedom of Information requests, knocking on doors of public institutions in New York such as schools and the City Council. It's interesting. The people in these places are still not used to a Spanish-speaking representative. One time, I was told I couldn't see a particular official because he had an appointment with a union representative. They didn't think the union rep that came to demonstrate awareness of the regulations and laws would be a Spanish speaker. Sometimes, though, I can get a lot of good information just talking to Spanish-speaking workers at a job site. I don't go in a suit and tie, and they are sympathetic to me and not so guarded. People from the same culture are more open and trusting.

When you speak only your native language, you are limited. After I learned English, I could understand a lot more of what was going on around me. Now my wife is taking English classes. My children are completely bilingual. My daughter needed a little extra help when she started in school, but she picked it up quickly from TV and other media. At home, we went from 100 percent Spanish to about 50–50 Spanish-English. Recently, we sent our son to Ecuador to help him to improve his Spanish! Thank God I was able to support my family for all those years without learning English, but if I had the tools then that I have now, I might have been able to get into a different position. Who knows?

At age 27, **BYRON SILVA** (Quito, Ecuador; 1968-) moved to the United States, where, as an abestos worker for a year, he earned enough to send for his wife and daughter. After six years of exposure to enough asbestos to lead him to expect serious health consequences when he is older, he joined a labor union and rose to shop steward. Silva is now a full-time union organizer. This is his first published work.

English Helped My Golf

– LORENA OCHOA –

I STARTED PLAYING GOLF at the age of five in my hometown of Guadalajara, Mexico. I played in my first state tournament at the age of six and I won my first national children's tournament at seven. It was thanks to my father that I learned to play. He encouraged me to practice and accompanied me to tournaments. My biggest surprise came when I won the chance to represent Mexico in a world tournament we played in San Diego, California. That was the best experience of my youth, and I'll never forget it. I was eight years old, and it was my first trip to the United States. We visited beautiful places, but sadly, we didn't speak English. It was at that point that I became determined to learn to speak the language so I could communicate with other players.

In San Diego I discovered that my golf game was very good and I could play against the best players in the world. When I returned home, I wanted to play golf every day to improve my game and travel to more tournaments. I practiced four hours after school every day, and I played in tournaments all over Mexico. Things were going well.

As I grew older, I played in tournaments in Mexico and, during the summer, in the United States. When I turned 17, my English was still not very good. That's when the University of Arizona offered me a scholarship. I very much wanted to go to Tucson and play golf for the university team, but I had to improve my English first. My initial attempt was at a school in Guadalajara. I didn't learn very much because I missed too many classes playing in out-of-town tournaments. As a result, I found a private teacher. It took me two years to learn English and pass the exams necessary to be accepted at the University of Arizona. One of the happiest moments of my life was when I learned that I had passed those tests.

The advice I would give about learning English is this: read a lot of magazines in English. That's how I expanded my vocabulary and learned grammar. We always did homework assignments based on magazine articles—that way you can keep abreast of what's going on in the world. The best magazines for this are fashion magazines as well as news magazines. Pay a lot of attention to how words are written. Equally important, read out loud to practice your pronunciation. Patience is key for everything you do, whether learning English or golf.

My two years of study at the University of Arizona were the best two years of my life. I learned a great deal, I played on the school's golf team, we won tournaments, and I matured as a person and as an athlete. Thanks to my experiences during those two years in Tucson, today I'm a better person and teammate and a better friend, sister, daughter, and golfer, too.

When I arrived at the university, I spoke English well, but not well enough to fully understand a college-level class. The first few months were difficult for me. With the help of tutors, I studied every afternoon. Watching movies in English became essential to understanding conversations at a normal pace as well as expanding my vocabulary. A good exercise, I discovered, was to watch a little bit of a movie with a friend or classmate, then to ask each other questions about what had happened and what was said. That helped enormously. It also helped me overcome my fear of talking with others and made me more confident to speak in public. I'm accustomed to golf terms in English, such as *birdie*, *bogey*, or *hole in one*. I always use the English vocabulary, but in Mexico we use both languages. You can say driver or *madera*, hole-in-one or *hoyo en uno*. Sometimes there is only an English word for a specific golf term, like *swing* or *putt*.

Being far from home is very hard, but when you know where you want to go and what your goals are, all those sacrifices are worthwhile. The most important thing is to be sure of yourself and to know what you want to achieve. I had many days of loneliness, sadness, anguish, and feeling defeated, but I also had days of joy, laughter, travel, tournament experience, and triumph that I wouldn't trade for anything.

To be honest, those two years at a university changed my life; I recommend that everyone seek that opportunity to travel and learn. Don't be afraid of being different. Decisions that are risky are the ones that give us back the most and are ultimately the most satisfying. Not speaking English is no excuse. You can achieve anything you set your mind to.

LORENA OCHOA (Guadalajara, Mexico; 1981-) is a top golfer in the Ladies Professional Golf Association. In an Associated Press poll of sportswriters, she was voted best female athlete for 2006. A recipient of Mexico's National Sports Award, she established a foundation in 2004 to advance sports and education opportunities for needy Mexican children.

My Stepmother Tongue

— PATRICIA DE SANTANA PINHO —

EACH LANGUAGE IS SPECIAL in its own way, but I must confess how fortunate I feel to have been born into the inventive Brazilian Portuguese, and how delicious it is to navigate in a language full of Bantu and Iorubá and Tupi-Guarani expressions that place the words in insubordinately arranged phrases. As a postcolonial language, Brazilian Portuguese is hybrid, daring, and resourceful, and full of secrets shared only by the postcolonized and by those who venture to slowly embark into this world.

But if Portuguese is the language of my thoughts, my feelings, and my dreams, it hasn't been so for my entire life. In fact, for three years of my childhood, English was actually my first language. And if today I can't think of it as a mother tongue, it was certainly a very good stepmother for me. I was almost eight years old when my parents moved to England in 1978 with their four children. After a few weeks, my younger sister Mari and I were basically "just speaking English" as if we had been doing so forever. At least that's how I remember it today. Until recently, I used to say that I did not remember how I learned English, but reflecting on this more carefully I realize that it was indeed a process, and not an instantaneous event. This is the fragmented and incomplete story of how I learned English.

My two older brothers had taken English classes before we left Brazil, but my little sister and I arrived in England without knowing a single word of the language. Yet, thanks to the freshness and flexibility of the almost wholesome minds of children, we learned

English immediately, or at least that's what our memory tells us. A few episodes, though, remind me that even children make infantile mistakes when learning a second language. When the teacher asked me which were my favorite shows on TV, I answered "Long Legs" and "Fat and Skinny," proud of my accurate translation of *Perna Longa* (Bugs Bunny), and *O Gordo e o Magro* (Laurel and Hardy).

While children's mistakes are acceptable, there is a lot less tolerance for the errors of adults, which is of course what makes it so difficult for them to learn a second language. Most grown-ups become embarrassed and feel that they look "child-like" when expressing wrong pronunciations, incorrect intonations, or unintended puns. My siblings and I would make so much fun of our parents and their "broken" English. But I also benefited from my Dad's clumsiness with the language. Helping me to pick an extra-curricular activity at school, he looked at the list and said: "You can choose among cooking, sewing, chess, and this other thing here which seems great: recorder. I think you will learn how to use a tape recorder." I immediately chose that, unaware at the time that I would turn out to be a researcher and that the tape recorder would become an important tool in my life. Needless to say that I was very confused when I arrived for my first "recorder" meeting and found out that it was in fact a music class. Because of my Dad's mix-up, I learned to play this instrument and was in love with it for a long time.

If speaking could be tricky, learning to write in English was even more challenging. I remember the first dictation at school: in my attempt to not miss one single word read aloud by the teacher, I wrote down absolutely everything she said, including the commas which I literally spelled on the paper, wondering what the heck that word meant, and why it was so excessively repeated throughout the teacher's story. Today, 28 years later, I have learned what *comma* means, though the proper way to employ it in the English language still remains a mystery to me.

Our pronunciation, on the other hand, was flawless: identical to that of our neighbors and classmates where we lived in the working-class area of Reading, about 50 miles west of London. Even the erasure of the "t" in words such as "thir-een," "four-een," and "wha-ever" made our intonation indistinguishable from the other kids. However, although our quick mastering of the language made it seem like we had been born there, we were constantly reminded that we had not. We were definitely not British. Someone must have taught the Brit kids to see us as "different." Boys yelled, "Brown girl, brown girl!" at me like a curse, then sped away from me, as if I would ever run after them.

What could possibly be wrong with being brown? I was, at the most, surprised with how much my brownness had any effect on them. In Brazil I was never considered *that* brown. Maybe it was the pinkness of *their* skin that emphasized the brownness of mine. My sister's kinky hair was the factor they elected to pick on. She was almost as light-skinned as they were, but with a very bushy hair that would defy the hairpins put in by my mom every morning with the hope that they would last all day. By midday the pins would have literally exploded from my sister's hair, flying away over the school's playground. This would drive her to tears on a bad day. And I would run to help her find an elastic band that would hold her hair at least until we arrived home in the afternoon.

Another "national" epithet used by my schoolmates to molest us was "Brazil Nut," probably the only reference to Brazil available to those little-informed inhabitants of the First World. Two years later, when we had moved 25 miles north to Oxford and were enrolled in another school, we came to understand that "nut" was a pejorative term for someone deemed crazy or wild. Maybe that idea went along with the other fantastic notions they had of Brazil since I was asked, every now and then, if my family and I lived in the jungle, if we had monkeys for pets, and if our means of transportation was swinging from creepers like Tarzan and Jane. Some children also dared to ask what adults could only wonder: "Do people in Brazil pee in the garden, or do you have loos?" Funny that they asked us if we had toilets when it seemed to us that they were the ones unaccustomed to showers.

It would be unfair if I left out the fond memories my family and I share of the three years we spent in England. They were incredibly special for our lives, and we often evoke our collective remembrances of that period. We laugh at the anecdotes that, for having been told and retold so many times, have acquired a life of their own. And we mourn in memory of some wonderful souls we had the fortune to make friends with while we were there, but which have already left this world. Ms. Randall is one of them, and I would like to record her name here as homage to this remarkable feminist who would make inflammatory speeches against British imperialism and drag us to protests against fox hunting, and who, like many other English folks we met, revealed an openness to getting to know us as regular human beings and did not see us as exotic creatures.

Today I actually regret the fact that I have lost a lot of my British accent. I can imagine how this may sound strange to my Caribbean friends who would probably, and with reason, associate a British accent with colonialism and domination. However, as for all languages, there are many British accents, and I miss not knowing anymore how to speak the working-class one I learned. Yet, watching a British movie, or talking with British friends for a few minutes is enough to resuscitate my childhood accent, or at least some invented version of it.

Living in the United States now, as a grown-up, I am aware of how learning a language is always an unfinished business. I am constantly and continuously learning how to speak, write, and read in English. While this brings me some uneasiness—especially in a context marked by a widespread lack of cosmopolitanism—there is always this pleasure of discovering new words and terms. For instance, the expression "to go there," meaning to figuratively revisit a memory or a feeling as if it were a place, is one that I learned only recently, and one which can describe what I am attempting in this essay. I find it not only very useful but also deeply poetic and beautiful. On the other hand, expressions such as "good for you" and the emphasis on words such as "winner" and "loser" bother me deep down in my soul as if they were screaming individualism and egocentrism. And there are accents, too, that can really drive me crazy, like that nasal way in which, "like," some high school and college American girls, "like," lethargically speak, probably believing it sounds sexy and trendy. Language is certainly a means through which gender operates to shape our beings.

It is quite revealing to look back at how I learned English and realize how much language is connected to feelings of nationality and to the predictable racial representations that are repetitively connected to nations. Then again, I must recognize that the way we articulate our memories reveals as much about our present as it does about our past. And the fact that I have been living for the last four years in a country that is possibly the most racialized in the world certainly shapes my past childhood recollections of living abroad.

None of us really remembers how we learned to speak the language we were born into. This tinges our relationship with our mother tongue not only with a lot of intimacy but also with a feeling that is almost magical, as if our language were innate to our beings. Defined as female, the mother tongue is imagined to breastfeed us our "native language," preparing us to actively inhabit our "fatherland." While rejecting all kinds of naturalizations, especially for the burden they impose on women and men and for the fixed gender roles they expect us to play, I believe there is a lot to be read, heard, and undone in these metaphors that bring together language, land, gender, and parenting.

The mother tongue is in fact like a parent: we do not choose it, yet we are, to a great extent, shaped by its expression and understanding of the world. As suggested by the dual meaning of the

Portuguese verb *criar*, we are both *created* and *raised* by our language. We may even, at times, reject our mother tongue, like silly adolescents who feel embarrassed by the presence of their caregivers, and seek the refuge or fanciness of other tongues, mothers of others, parents of the cool friends we look up to when we're still too immature to value what life has chosen to give us. Stepmother tongues are, thus, disruptive and rebellious since they break automatic associations and overturn unquestioned expectations.

Having learned English at such an early age has significantly favored my siblings and me in both professional and practical terms. Each one of us today still harvests the fruits of our past experience abroad. But it has above all enhanced our ability to look at the world in a much broader and interconnected manner. If languages have been appropriated by national projects, they can also disobey physical and symbolic frontiers and express the shared feelings of our common human condition.

PATRICIA DE SANTANA PINHO (Salvador da Bahia, Brazil; 1970-) is an assistant professor in the Department of Latin American, Caribbean, and U.S. Latino Studies at the State University of New York at Albany. Her forthcoming book is *Reinventing Africa in Bahia*, to be followed by one on African-American roots of tourism to Brazil. Previously, Pinho was a lecturer at Yale University and a Mellon Fellow in the Department of Black Studies at Amherst College.

From Basic Training to Fluent English

— JOSÉ BAJANDAS —

I WAS BORN ON April 26, 1920, on Vieques, a small island off the eastern coast of Puerto Rico. Outsiders recently learned of Vieques during the controversy between locals and the U.S. Navy. The Navy occupied two-thirds of the island for joint maneuvers with the navies of foreign countries and stored bombs and ammunitions there as well.

My father was a self-made bookkeeper who worked in a sugar factory on Vieques. My mother was a housewife during my youth. They were middle-class Puerto Ricans of Spanish descent and consequently I spoke and wrote only in Spanish during my younger years. I also have two brothers and two sisters. I remember very clearly my father trying to speak English to an American worker at the sugar factory. Not knowing too much English he would gesture, combine words in Spanish with English, and mimic the American accent.

At age five, my family moved to Mayagüez, my mother's birthplace, more than a hundred miles from Vieques at the other end of Puerto Rico. My primary and secondary education took place there, and it was there that I learned my first English words, through a rhyme:

Pollito chicken, *gallina* hen
lápiz pencil, and *pluma* pen.

I also learned the sentence "I am hungry."

I graduated from the commercial course at Mayagüez High School in July 1940. There I learned basic grammar. I remember my teacher, Madeline Williamson, who later became a renowned Puerto Rican actress. Since she was American, all the classes were conducted in English, and we had to have a sharp ear to determine what she had to say. She was an excellent teacher, and I enjoyed attending her classes.

After graduating from high school, I looked for a job as stenographer and bookkeeper. During those recession years, work was very scarce in Puerto Rico. Unable to secure gainful employment I decided to sign up in the U.S. Army National Guard. Up until 1940 my training in English had been very limited, and for this reason my spoken and written English was poor. I enlisted as a private in Company B, 130th Engineers (Combat). This unit was composed of Puerto Ricans, and we usually spoke Spanish.

A short time later I was promoted to staff sergeant to act as platoon leader. I held that post until September 1942, when I was selected to attend the Officer Candidate School in Fort Benning, Georgia. From September 1942 to January 1943 I completed the officer candidate course at the U.S. Army Infantry School and achieved the rank of 2nd lieutenant.

We were taught basic military terminology in classes of about 150 students, all in English. My classmates were all native English speakers. When we were called upon to make oral presentations on military subjects, such as the use of the bayonet in combat fighting, we had to do them in English, of course. Later, I attended the Army Chemical Warfare School to complete a course to become a regimental gas officer. Here, classes were smaller, and we were required to participate daily. Again, all my classmates were American officers. We socialized at the Officers Club, where I continued my daily practice of English.

These experiences opened many other opportunities for me, such as becoming 1st lieutenant, captain, and later major in the U.S. Army Reserve. To attain these positions, I had to complete additional military training. These classes were conducted in English by American instructors, giving me the opportunity to continue learning and polishing my English. In my everyday duties I had to supervise other investigators, correcting their reports for content, completeness, format, and grammar. This work helped me acquire an even better understanding and use of the English language.

In July 1955 I moved to Chicago with my family. As captain at the time, I had the privilege of living inside the Army facilities. My neighbors were all English-speaking, and my daughters attended school in English. I was required to speak English daily, at work as well as in social situations. This experience made me think in English. I usually think in English now, and when I write in Spanish, I have to watch myself because I tend to use English rather than Spanish.

I believe that the following factors contributed to my learning of the English language:

1. The interest and desire to learn a second language awakened by seeing, as a child, my father trying to speak a second language
2. Being exposed and listening to English during my elementary school
3. Having an excellent teacher, Ms. Madeline Williamson, in high school
4. Attending the different service schools during my military career, where I had English-speaking instructors and classmates
5. My close daily association with English speakers every day during my 20 years of active military service
6. Reading English books, magazines, and newspapers daily

Today, I look back at my life experiences with satisfaction. I graduated in 1965 magna cum laude from the Business Administration Program at the University of Puerto Rico, Río Piedras campus. I have been able to support my wife who became an English teacher and later went back to school to complete a degree as a librarian.

I have two lovely daughters, both college-educated professionals, who grew up in a bilingual environment. Thinking back, I could not imagine, as a kid growing up in Mayagüez, the chain of events that followed that first simple rhyme:

Pollito chicken, *gallina* hen
lápiz pencil, and *pluma* pen.

JOSÉ BAJANDAS (Vieques, Puerto Rico; 1920-2007), who retired as a U.S. Army major after 20 years' service, was a member of the Military Officers Association of America, the Commanders Club of the Disabled American Veterans, and the National Association for Uniformed Service. Additionally, he was a member of the Puerto Rico Museum of Art and enjoyed reading, dancing, and tending his garden.

The Secret Language

– DAISY ZAMORA –

THE FIRST WORDS I HEARD in English were from my grandmother Ilse Gámez, who I remember as a magical presence in my childhood. Everything about her seemed legendary to me. Among the stories she used to tell, my favorites were about her life in New Orleans, where she and her family arrived from Europe and where she spent her childhood until she was 14, when they set sail again, bound for Nicaragua, fulfilling her parents' wish to return definitively to their country of origin. Her stories of New Orleans were filled with references and names in English (frequently also in French), and those mysterious words, so different from the ones I heard in everyday speech, produced in me an irresistible fascination. They sounded like strange music, an exotic melody coming from faraway fantastic places where life had an agitation, a rhythm, an acceleration unknown and unheard-of in the peaceful world I shared with my parents, sisters, and brothers. We were all part of an enormous family that included grandparents, great-aunts, great-uncles, uncles, aunts, and first cousins, as well as a second and third level of blood relatives, followed immediately by all the other people in the category of relatives included in the family universe and its state of perpetual expansion.

The English I heard from my grandmother Ilse had nothing to do with the English I was taught in kindergarten through songs teaching us to count from one to ten, or the language that appeared in the English textbooks we studied in the second and third grade of primary school: *See Dick. See Jane. See Spot. See Puff. See Spot run. See Puff jump.* For me, that English lacked charm, instead sounding like the noise of my shoes crunching in the gravel of the schoolyard during recess. But that other English, the one my grandmother and her sisters spoke, possessed multiple and varied registers that always amazed me. Sometimes it sounded like the trill of a bird, light and crystalline, and at other times flowed in dense, thick amber like honey. It would rise in high notes with the lonely, nostalgic sound of a transverse flute or swirl in a whirlpool like the frenzied crowds I imagined rushing around the streets of a big metropolis.

But they spoke English only among themselves, in their private conversations, never in front of other people, especially if one of those people was my grandfather Vicente, who seemed to view English as an offense to his personal dignity and Nicaragua's integrity. Since the middle of the 19th century, too many interventions by successive U.S. governments had occurred in Nicaraguan history not to have their bitter consequences extended to the language, contaminating it for many Nicaraguans as the odious tongue of an invader whose supreme act of cruelty was to withdraw the Marines from our country and leave us with an installed dictator President Franklin Delano Roosevelt cleverly described: *He may be a son of a bitch, but he's our son of a bitch.* Those words were known by all Nicaraguans, circulated by word of mouth in the original English. That dictator, at the service of U.S. interests and not our country's, initiated a repressive, bloodthirsty family dynasty that the Nicaraguan people suffered under from 1936 to July 19, 1979, the date the last representative of the dictatorship was overthrown by a popular and massive revolution.

There was, then, a sort of tacit censorship, an inexplicit taboo, surrounding the secret language through which my great-aunts and my grandmother communicated, and which attracted me with the power and charm of something forbidden: the apple offered in the Garden of Eden. On the other hand, the English we studied in class didn't seem to bother anyone. Instead, it was approved of, and we repeated it in unison, almost shouting, the nuns constantly encouraging us to practice it in conversation. I perceived the dichotomy and accepted it as something natural among the experiences that were part of my everyday life.

Before long, my ears began to discern another way of speaking the language. It was not the cryptic and fantastic English full of attractions and mystery that I loved to listen to, nor the tiresome, repetitious one that sounded like a cart struggling over cobbled streets. No, this other English expressed things in a different way that was not enigmatic and seductive, nor dumb and monotonous, but dramatic and direct: whatever the characters said, happened simultaneously. That is to say, a word was an act; words and action occurred at the same time. An activity was named at the very moment it took place. For example, a character that was evidently crying, would say: *I'm crying*. Another one, obviously hiding something, would declare: *I'll hide this!*

It was the English I started to learn from cartoons on television, where the characters expressed thoughts, emotions, and feelings in a straightforward way: *Out! Help! Stop it! Don't go away! I'll be back! Let's go!* I learned phrases and words that communicated necessity in a fast, precise manner. The language of cartoons also introduced me to metaphors. The first time I heard characters in a downpour shouting their heads off with the phrase, *"The sky is falling, the sky is falling!"* I believed it was the proper way to say in English, "It's a downpour," or "It's raining very hard."

I had no choice but to learn yet another kind of English from cowboy movies, because my cousins constantly used it in their games. Also, in a mechanical way, I learned by heart the English names for all the plays in baseball, the most popular sport in Nicaragua.

The hidden reluctance my grandfather bore toward English for historical and political reasons, and because of his way of understanding national dignity, did not interfere in any way with his understanding that, as part of our education and acquisition of culture, it was important for us to learn the language. I don't remember him ever saying a word against our studying it, or exhibiting any displeasure that my parents enrolled my sisters and me at Saint Theresa's Academy, a bilingual school that was Spanish-English in the elementary grades, augmented by French in high school.

Gradually the English that was so dull to me in the first grades of school expanded and deepened with readings transforming it into a beautiful language that kept growing inside, becoming more and more a part of my consciousness, invading my thoughts and appearing in my dreams. Understanding the language and speaking it in a natural way became integral to my being, my way of appreciating literature, especially poetry, and enjoying the lyrics of my favorite songs, which I was able to repeat perfectly.

Literature classes were my favorite. To act as a character in any of Shakespeare's plays, or to read an O. Henry short story out loud to my classmates, or a chapter of Robert Louis Stevenson's *Treasure Island*, or a sonnet by Elizabeth Barrett Browning, brightened my day. At the school library, I discovered, among other authors, Walt Whitman, Emily Dickinson, and Edna St. Vincent Millay, then Carl Sandburg and William Carlos Williams. Further along, I encountered William Blake, the sisters Brönte, Jane Austen, and Ernest Hemingway. Years later, while at university, I read the Americans William Faulkner, Ezra Pound, and Gertrude Stein, and the Irish authors William Butler Yeats and James Joyce.

Along with my intense reading, I also became a music lover and put together a rather substantial collection of Frank Sinatra and Beatles records—my favorites, although my interests included many other groups and singers in English. From that deep relationship with the language, I wound up with what I considered a broad and complex knowledge of English, the sounds of which captivated me in the first years of life.

But my true encounter with living English (that is, the one spoken in everyday life) happened in the United States, where I went to spend my school vacations in Middletown, Connecticut. My first impression of the country was completely idyllic. My aunt and uncle's house, where I would stay for three months, was a beautiful and comfortable three-story building, an old New England manor with a gorgeous garden out back, an orchard, a stable with horses, and a pond full of trout. A dense woods of birch and a variety of pine and spruce trees, crisscrossed by narrow paths dotted with wildflowers, went around the edge of that peaceful pond in a landscape that seemed like it was lifted from a fairy tale. Those vacations are part of the happy memories of my life because I also had the unforgettable experience of going to New York City for the first time and visiting the 1964 World's Fair. However, what is most deeply imprinted in my memory of that first visit to the U.S. is the shock I received from the language I had believed I understood and spoke correctly.

Almost immediately, I realized that my English, that is, the English through which I expressed myself, sounded strange to everybody. My cousins, not to mention their friends, listened to me with surprise or mocking looks. In turn, their English was almost unintelligible to me because they spoke, of course, in teenage slang. When one of my cousins couldn't stand it anymore, she told me that I was a weirdo, that I spoke like a philosopher, some sort of Socrates or something, and asked me to make an effort to try to talk like normal people so I could make some friends. She didn't have a clue about the extreme anguish I was going through trying to understand what was being said around me, trying to decipher everything I misunderstood, assuming one thing for another. Desolated, I thought about the abundant literature I had read up to then, and the songs I had worked so hard to memorize. It was all worthless for learning to speak practical English that would help me establish bonds with boys and girls my own age. On the contrary, the vocabulary I learned from books, especially from the poetry that taught me to love the language, had no place in the everyday speech of my contemporaries.

To be accepted by everybody, I started paying extreme attention to how I expressed myself and to the words I chose. I anxiously searched for ways to adapt my way of speaking, imitating what I heard from others, so I wouldn't be excluded from their conversations or activities. I understood that if I didn't do that, I would be left on the fringes of the main current, the mainstream where all U.S. teenagers lived, with space only for themselves. The barrier was not easy to cross, and when I couldn't do it, my consolation was to take refuge in the library of the house, where I read, during that first vacation, an English translation of Fyodor Dostoevsky's *Crime and Punishment.*

I was 14 years old when I went to the States for the first time—the same age as my grandmother Ilse when she watched New Orleans fade into the distance from the deck of a steamship—and ever since then I've understood what it means to *live* in direct contact with a language through the people who speak it, through their culture, and through their vision of the world.

Poet **DAISY ZAMORA** (Managua, Nicaragua; 1950-) has authored five books of poetry including *The Violent Foam, Riverbed of Memory,* and *Clean Slate.* She fought with Nicaragua's National Sandinista Liberation Front during that country's successful revolution, and served as vice minister of Culture in the new government. Her homeland has awarded her many prizes, including Woman Writer of the Year (2006) and the Mariano Fiallos Gil National Poetry Prize. In California, she won a state Arts Council Fellowship for poetry, and was a featured artist in the Bill Moyers PBS series *The Language of Life.*

Fluid, Dynamic, and Mischievous

— MIGUEL BARNET —

WORDS ENTERED WITH BLOOD. At eight years old I was thrown very suddenly into a North American school in Cuba, not knowing a word of English. All classes at Cathedral School were taught in English. If I uttered a single word in Spanish, it cost me a nickel, which I had to deposit in the collection box.

What English I know, I learned by force, but I learned it well and I speak it with a good deal of fluency. I love the language of Shakespeare and Faulkner; it is beautiful, fluid, synthetic, and it has helped me greatly to make my way in the world. It has made me more cosmopolitan.

Music helped a great deal. In school we would sing rounds, which I still know by heart. In the school's Episcopal church, I sang religious hymns, too, with my beautiful voice, and that sent me on an ego trip on which I still travel.

I made great efforts to watch movies in English without looking at the subtitles, and that helped a lot. I must also confess that in my adolescence I had many North American friends in Cuba, with whom I shared my teenage years at the Community House, at the Mother's Club, and in the school's Parish House.

I speak English every day and I read a great deal of English as well, to keep it alive and up to date. What a dynamic language! We will never learn it completely, because it is mischievous and ever more challenging and unreachable.

My ear saved me, allowing me to capture the richness of English. Literature opened the way for me to enter more deeply into its mystery.

When I discovered that I could speak for three days straight in the language I learned by bloodshed, I sang out:

Hark, the herald angels sing! Glory to the newborn king!

MIGUEL BARNET (Havana, Cuba; 1940-) is a poet, novelist, screenwriter, and ethnographer. His books include the internationally published *Biography of a Runaway Slave* and *Song of Rachel*, as well as numerous volumes of poetry. He has served as Cuba's representative to UNESCO, and in 2006 he was awarded the Juan Rulfo International Prize for his novella *Fatima o el Parque de Fraternidad* (*Fatima or the Brotherhood Park*). He is currently president of the Fernando Ortiz Cultural Foundation in Havana, where he is a member of Cuba's National Assembly.

My Tongue Is Divided into Two

— QUIQUE AVILES —

I WORSHIPPED THE ENGLISH language before I understood it. As far back as I can remember, the promise of English was part of my life.

The first words in the English language that I remember hearing were: "Pan Am Airlines." That was the airline that used to take my mother away from El Salvador and then bring her back again from the United States. The next word I remember was "Sheraton," the Washington, D.C. hotel where my mother worked in the laundromat for 25 years. In 1969, when I was four, my mother borrowed money from her mother to travel to the United States as a tourist. Her real intention was to stay in the States, get a good job, and offer her children a better life. She made a promise to bring us, her four children, one by one—starting with the oldest and ending with the youngest, which was me. With that promise came the promise that English would be a part of my life.

> My tongue is divided into two
> by virtue, coincidence or heaven
> words jumping out of my mouth
> stepping on each other
> enjoying being a voice for the message
> expecting conclusions…

I've learned English in three different phases.

Phase One: *Curiosity and Wonder*

Having a mother who was in the United States meant that my brothers, my sister, and I got American gifts with words in English each time she came home. One of my favorites was a bag full of plastic cowboys and Indians that came with a cowboy-and-Indian-themed coloring book with English captions underneath each picture. I would sit with a dictionary and struggle to make out a few words so I could know more about my mother's new world.

In the mid-1970s, the Salvadoran Education Department brought "Televisión Educativa" to schools across the country. With it, came televised English classes with Mr. Mayorga, an upbeat, well-dressed teacher with near-perfect control of his facial muscles. "Good morning, children. I am Mr. Mayorga." It was Mr. Mayorga who first introduced me to the concept of pronunciation and the need to use certain facial muscles to achieve specific sounds. He would demonstrate the sound of a hard *t* by holding a wire hoop to his mouth. The hoop had strips of paper that would flap as he repeated "Good nighttttt…Good nighttttt." But Mr. Mayorga and his scientific techniques did not prepare me for the complexities of the *th* sound. It would take me many more years to correctly pronounce "thirty."

my tongue is divided into two
into heavy accent bits of confusion
into miracles and accidents
saying things that hurt the heart
drowning in a language that lives, jumps, translates…

Like most kids anywhere in the world, American music and television were also my English teachers. But it was the desire to be cool—more that the desire to learn English—that fed the infatuation with these exotic American exports. My family was only the second family in our whole town to own a television. English poured out of our house. My grandmother would charge five cents for people from the town to sit on our tile floor watching a black-and-white 19-inch TV. *The Three Stooges*, *Tarzan*, the World Cup, and Mohammad Ali fights were the big sellers. Late at night I would watch *Kojak*, *Mission: Impossible*, and *Starsky and Hutch*—swallowing up English, aspiring to be cool, and knowing that my mother had my ticket on layaway.

In late 1978, I had a political awakening. My country was ruled by the military and their martial law against ideas. I was 13 years old and joined the student movement. We demanded books, chalk, better teachers, and cleaner bathrooms. In the revolutionary fervor of those days, the coolness of English was ruined by Marx and Lenin. The language that fed my wonder and curiosity was now, according to my comrades, the language of the enemy, of Yankee Imperialism. It was no longer cool. The next thing I knew, I was on a plane to the United States to save me from the death squads.

> My tongue is divided by nature
> by our crazy desire to triumph and conquer
> this tongue is cut up into equal pieces
> one wants to curse and sing out loud
> the other one simply wants to ask for water…

Phase Two: *Frustration and Need (How English Became My Imperial Liberator)* In the fall of 1980, Ronald Reagan was elected president and I started 9th grade at Francis Junior High in Washington, D.C. Kids from Central America were coming into the school in droves every week. We were thrown into English as a Second language (ESL) classes where Mrs. Padrino taught us that the heart of the English language is the verb "to be." We learned to say, "Hello, how are you today? I am fine, thank you," in crisp English. On weekends, I went to rallies and protests—ESL classes for leftists. There, I got to repeat "No draft, no war / US out of El Salvador!" and "We demand the truth, about El Salvador!" over and over again.

My mother was renting a house at 14th and Irving, the black section of El Barrio. We had a neighbor, an older black man, who was always outside tending his garden, wearing overalls and speaking in a Southern drawl. He would smile at me and say something that sounded like, "hayalldoin." I would turn to my older brother, Pedro, and ask him, "What did he say?" My brother would answer, "He asked you how you're doing." And I would respond, "Isn't that supposed to be, 'Hello, how are you?'" This was not the crisp English of my ESL teachers.

By this time, I was beginning to understand that English was not just one language. At school, I became friends with Pichi, a chubby white Puerto Rican who came to D.C. via New Jersey. Pichi spoke three languages: Puerto Rican Spanish (which I barely understood), formal English (which I was beginning to understand), and Black English (which I now understood I needed to learn in order to survive). Pichi became my real ESL teacher.

tongue
English of the funny sounds
tongue
funny sounds in English
tongue
sounds funny in English
tongue
in funny English sounds

It was Pichi who gave me a copy of *Puerto Rican Obituary*, a poetry book by Pedro Pietri, one of the first and most influential of the Nuyorican poets of the 1970s. I had been writing poetry since I was ten years old, mainly rhyming, cheesy love poems. This book changed my life. It changed how I learned English, how I understood it, and what I could do with it. It introduced me to the possibility of words as a weapon. I started mixing my anger, my Spanish, and my limited English into poetry. My first attempts were long diatribes that were more political than poetic. But English began to feel good. I began to feel that it was something I could use as revenge.

When it was time for me to start high school, I decided to audition for the Theater Department at the Duke Ellington School of the Arts. With my angry, broken English, I made an impression and got in. My first year was very hard. I was the only Latino in the whole school of more than 400 students. Rosemary Walsh, my acting teacher, would tell me, "You're a good actor, but I can't understand what the fuck you're saying. We're gonna work on you." My teachers were convinced my success as an actor required the removal of my accent. My second year at Ellington, I was assigned to speech classes. We studied phonetics and the anatomy of our sound-making factory: the mouth, the throat, the vocal chords, and the diaphram. These classes consisted of repetitive speech exercises, such as:

"Theophilus thistle, the unsuccessful thistle sifter, while sifting a sieve of unsifted thistles thrusts three thousand thistles through the thick of his thumb…"

"Unique New York, Unique New York, Unique New York…"

"One hundred ninety-nine nuns in an Indiana nunnery…"

So, here I was, thinking that I was making so much progress with my English, I could move to New York or L.A. and make it big.

my tongue is divided into two
a border patrol runs through the middle
frisking words
asking for proper identification
checking for pronunciation…

By my senior year I had become a punk rocker, a combat-boot wearing rebel. I realized that there were no parts for me in traditional theater, that if I wanted to be an actor, I would have to write my own parts. With that realization, I began a deeper, artistic relationship with the English language. My new teachers became Nikki Giovanni, June Jordan, Lucille Clifton, and Alice Walker—black writers who were using language to say that we are beautiful, that we deserve things. I began to write monologues for characters that came from my life. As I began to develop my own voice, English became my imperial liberator.

Phase Three: *Subtlety and Payback*
I am still learning English. *El inglés.* Sometimes, in the middle of a performance, my mispronunciation of a word will throw a shadow on its meaning. A reference to the New Mexican desert comes across as a reference to *sopapillas*. Once, I introduced a young writer as a "jewel." Later, several people came up to me and asked, "Why did you have to mention that she's Jewish?"

As one of my characters says, "English is the language of offense and cordiality." It keeps coming at me. I keep learning how to handle it, tame it, seduce it, make it work to my advantage. Sometimes, it refuses. I have been trying for five years to write a piece about the many people who live inside me: the Mayan, the Spaniard, the Latin. I know this piece will eventually happen, but I don't know when. Thoughts flow to me in Spanish, in Spanglish, and in Ingleñol. And yet, in just English, the words won't budge.

Since the mid-1980s I have been writing and performing one-person shows that weave together poetry and monologues in English. Latinos often ask me, "Why don't you do more in Spanish?" I often respond, "Because you all don't pay my rent." But the real answer is: payback. I use English to challenge English speakers to question their assumptions about us Latinos, about each other, and, in these xenophobic times, about immigrants in general. I use it to poke, prod, question, and make people feel uncomfortable. I always read my poems from a music stand (I have very few of them memorized), and whenever I leave my house for a gig, carrying my music stand to the car, I always feel that I am carrying my *machete*. Words are my weapon.

They are also the way I build alliances. I have learned that building trust with someone who is different from you in this country is all about mastering their own version of the English language. Most of my work in D.C. has been with black kids. I go into classrooms and use theater improvisation as a tool for encouraging kids to write about their lives. Most kids want to do improvs about drugs and guns, the thug life. I challenge them by asking, "Does your momma love you? Do you smile? Do you laugh? Are there tender moments in your life?" For the majority of kids, the answer is yes. So I challenge them to create skits about those soft and tender moments and then to write poetry about it. I challenge them not to fulfill society's expectations of poor kids by being drug dealers and thugs. And I always tell them, "Ain't nobody gonna sing our song, so we might as well sing it ourselves."

For me, learning English has been about learning to sing my own song.

my tongue is divided into two
my tongue is divided into two
I like my tongue
it says what feels right
I like my tongue
it says what feels right

QUIQUE AVILES (Sonsonate, El Salvador; 1965-) is a Washington, D.C.-based poet and performance artist. He is the author of *The Immigrant Museum*, and his one-man shows include *Caminata: A Walk Through Immigrant America*, *Chaos Standing/El Caos de Pie*, and *Salvatrucans*. Aviles' work has been broadcast on National Public Radio and performed at many colleges and community centers. He is a recipient of the Washington Mayor's Arts Award.

part three

You taught me language; and my
profit on't Is, I know how to curse

–Caliban, in *The Tempest*
by William Shakespeare

The Blessings of Arroz con Mango

– CRISTINA SARALEGUI –

I WAS ONLY 11 YEARS OLD when my family arrived in the United States and settled in Key Biscayne, Florida, a small, tropical island linked to Miami by a causeway. At that time, we were one of the only Spanish-speaking families on the island. I was placed in a nuns' school called the Assumption Academy. Now mind you, prior to this, the extent of my English education was what I heard while watching American TV in Cuba. Before any of us even dreamed that we would be fleeing the island because of Fidel, I was a big fan of American programs, especially the ones with Hopalong Cassidy, Roy Rogers, and Gene Autry. I watched them so much that I knew their lines better than they did. My favorite show featured a character called the Black Whip. I just loved that show! I would dress up all in black, scarf included, just like the Black Whip.

So there I was, the new student at the Assumption Academy. The nuns sized me up with their measuring stares, determining just how much molding this little piece of clay would require. So, I quickly called on the lessons of my childhood English professors—Hopalong, Roy, Gene, and the Black Whip—and gave the nuns the best I had to offer.

"Stick 'em up!"

Well, as you can imagine, the nuns really didn't appreciate that. They knew that in order to expand my English skills beyond the necessary phrases for shootouts and bank holdups, I was going to require more than some slight molding. Believe me, it was more of a major overhaul, as they set out to help me master English as quickly as possible.

As time passed, I grew more accustomed to my new home and language. Ironically, by the time I was offered an internship at *Vanidades* (a Spanish-language fashion and lifestyle magazine) during my senior year of college, I faced the startling realization that, after all my years in the United States, I had actually forgotten how to write Spanish correctly! I had to quickly teach myself all over again in order to succeed at my internship.

I guess all of this intermingling over the years of my English and Spanish has resulted in my unique style of communicating on TV and in print. I come from the *arroz con mango* school of communication—"rice and mango" being Cuban slang for hodge-podge. There are many Hispanic Americans in Miami who are fully bilingual. The side effect of this is a phenomenon called "Spanglish," where one can switch back and forth between English and Spanish multiple times in one sentence! Bilingual Miamians are so used to speaking Spanglish that when one has to actually speak all English or all Spanish it doesn't come out all that naturally.

My Spanglish has made me go through unusual and sometimes embarrassing moments, such as the time I approached a department store makeup counter with the intention of asking for *cedro* (cedar) eyeshadow. I can still see the look on the attendant's face when I mixed up the pronunciation and asked for "cheddar" eyeshadow. She didn't know if my English was poor or if I was trying to set a new cosmetics trend by lining my eyes with a block of aged cheese.

My Spanglish can be tough on my kids, too. We all embarrass our kids a little from time to time, but when I'm speaking with my daughter's American husband and in-laws and my daughter shoots me that "that-word-doesn't-even-exist" look, well, it's at those moments that I feel like my friend Charo!

All puns, mispronunciations, and invented words aside, I feel blessed for the opportunity I've had to learn English and be a part of this wonderful country that welcomed my family with open arms. I am as proud to be an American as I am of my Cuban heritage. God bless America!

CRISTINA SARALEGUI (Havana, Cuba; 1948-) has won twelve Emmys, the "Gracie Allen Tribute" from the Foundation of American Women in Radio and Television, and the Hispanic Heritage Arts Award for her Univision program, *Cristina*. She has addressed the United Nations in support of AIDS research and served on the board of the National Council of the American Foundation for AIDS Research. Cristina is a recipient of the Simon Weisenthal Center International Distinguished Achievement Award, and the author of *My Life as a Blonde*.

Who Knew Desi Arnaz Wasn't White?

— H. G. CARRILLO —

CUBAN VANITIES— a *tía* will now say while another nods and a third clicks her tongue *sí*–"runned a-fevered" in Miami's Havana Pequeña in the early 1970s. Back then, my mother and each of her sisters had a story about being told to "Speak English!" when she thought that she already was. Most of the tías only shopped in *cubano* stores, refusing to be women who took a second-grader around with them to translate. They all knew somebody who had been duped, cheated, or swindled, and if you know anything about the enormity of the ego of feminine *cubanidad*…uh…well…*es entendido*. "We camed to this country to make it work," they will all tell you.

Nearly ten years after the CIA-led invasion at La Playa Girón, as much as there was to preserve, there was twice as much to reinvent. This was before infomercials offered English fluency in a package of 12 CDs and a workbook, with a six-month guarantee of fun *para la familia entera* for 20 easy payments of $29.99 or your money back.

There were no bilingual instructions on busses or in elevators, no Spanish-speaking operators or ATMs, no Spanish-labeled aisles in supermarkets marked "Ethnic Foods" or "Ethnic Hair Care" where one can find bilingual shampoo and the lotion/*loción* the sisters swear makes their skin softer and smoother than its monolingual equivalents.

Then, if what came over a desk or a counter was halting, heavily accented, or misconjugated, there was no shortage of simple solutions like, "Learn the language; you're in America now!" A nun told my mother, because I wouldn't talk, that she believed that I was retarded and hypothesized that the reason was that Spanish was spoken in the home.

Exilos, refugees, displacements—there were dozens of names for those of us who came from Cuba at the time—were still receiving the welcoming benefits of the arms of the Cuban Relief Program (CRP). Job placement services, centers that provided regular meals and relocation information, the CRP was responsible for finding requalification training for professionals as well as finding a great deal of the legal aid that everyone thought they needed.

You went to the CRP offices if you were looking for relatives or didn't have a sponsor. They found housing for my parents, my sisters, my cousins; three of my mother's sisters and their parents, and *abuelo's* two fighting cocks—Tarzán and Mongo—so that we were all together in the four apartments, the entire first floor, with our noise, our Spanish, our cooking, the scatter of toys, and chicken droppings in public housing.

And it was someone associated with CRP who also provided us with the 1964 Magnavox Model 552 Color TV. I remember the make and model number quite clearly for—after a few months of school—the number of times that I ran my finger under the escutcheon to show a younger cousin that it really wasn't a "box" like everyone else in the family said, but a "vox." "V, vuh, like in vine," I would repeat the way my teacher did, yet to this day, if you are driving with him in his "ban" and he hears a song that he likes my cousin will ask you to "turn up the bolume, man."

But it was indeed a box. Long and rectangular, a wood veneer cabinet on spindly legs. Inside there was a Hi-Fi System that had a broken tone-arm, so my cousins and I would set the turntable to 45 and race our Hot Wheels.

It came with only one LP, and when my tía Rita took the jacketless copy of Iron Butterfly's In-A-Gadda-Da-Vida to have the title translated at the CRP, whatever she was told caused her to throw it away. Something evil I suppose, that necessitated a second burning of white sage and throwing of the divining shells; the first had been performed outside in the courtyard of the building before my mother and her sisters allowed the Vox to rest along the wall in front of the Hide-a-Bed where I slept with my cousins Julio and Enrique.

Nearly 24 hours a day for the two years that we were all living there together, it was on. My cousins and I learned to sleep through my *tíos* yelling boxers and baseball players to victory, and we adjusted to coming home from school to find our mothers passing tissues in front of *telenovelas*.

From races—bicycle, downhill, driving—we learned to say, "And they're off" with the announcer. *The French Chef* taught us to start meals with "Bon appetit!" We knew the lyrics to theme songs of *Gilligan's Island* and *Green Acres* without even knowing what they meant. *The Morning News* and *The Evening News*, and *The Mid-Day News Report*. *The Three Stooges*, *The Flintstones*, and *The Jetsons*. It was always on. My mother and tías Rita, Anita, y Dolores insisted, and we all, including mis abuelos, my father and all the tíos, capitulated.

Sí, my mother and her sisters were the plaiters of hair, laundresses, maids, and cooks; they arbitrated fights, bandaged the scrapes, and doled out the smacks on the backs of the heads. But also, each brassiere was a bank account that enabled us to get through the week as well as have an occasional ice cream. The papers that made us legal were kept in pots, under ice trays in freezers, and were slipped into the panels of girdles unused even on the Sundays when the sisters straightened ties and hair ribbons, cleaned the grime off with spittle, corrected postures with the whack of a handbag, and held us all together.

Alarm clocks and seamstresses, they clipped coupons and repaired frayed cords on appliances before they sent their men off to drive cabs, shuck oysters, haul fish, and can fruit. They spent a large part of their days shuffling from office to office, filling out the forms that got their husbands into classes, enrolled them into programs that would requalify them for the types of jobs, the kinds of careers, they had left in Cuba.

To all of us, the sisters were fearless out in a world that made my father and uncles weary and silent. The same environment that sent my father to stand in the shower, and my tío Tudy to slump over a beer in the kitchen, and my tío Chucho to fall asleep sitting up with his clothes on, and made los abuelos silent and small, invigorated the sisters. They taught each other the quickest routes, the most convenient bus stops, and instructed us kids who were over ten to say we were seven or eight so we could ride for free, and to say things like "Tell them 'I will not!' *como* Ann Marie on *That Girl*."

They took temperatures with the backs of their hands and taught us to say "I see" like Shana Alexander instead of nodding, "because it made you seem smarter while you were thinking what to say next." While rolling pennies, they could rattle off the phone numbers of government offices and extensions that would connect directly with someone who spoke Spanish. But what brought English into our home was that they were great collectors of *chismes* and cognates.

Thick as the smell from frying garlic and onions between those four apartments was the concern for learning to speak English well that nobody talked about because no one was really sure how we were going to go about it. "E-specially for you kids," one tía will say now, and another will nod and click her tongue, "Sí, we wanted all of you to talk real nice and have chances."

And it was by chance that my tía Rita discovered that if she watched como Mrs. Kravitz on *Bewitched* and told what she knew about a certain married greengrocer and a nurse, the man who fitted all of us kids for shoes spent a good part of the afternoon showing us that *zapatos* and shoes were the same thing. And we learned that though *zapatos tenis* were tennis shoes, what we call *zapatillos* were something else and we should just call them *shoes*. Rita recalled he told us the holes were called *eyelets*, *cordones/laces*, and the flap was a *tongue* just like the *tongue* in our mouths. "That little man just sat there on his little chair," recounted Rita, "waiting like Floyd the Barber on *The Andy Griffith Show* for me to tell him more."

At a *botanica*, tía Anita quietly alerted the owner to a woman stealing in the back of the store, after which each time she went in, she came out with more English to pass along over dinner. It's how we learned that *cambio* was *change*, "*Como una ché*," the woman told her, "ché-a-n-n-g-e."

They sang "Que sera, sera" and threw their heads like Doris Day on her short-lived situation comedy when people tried to take advantage of them, or ignored them in line, or pretended not to understand what they were saying. We kids were encouraged to say "Yes sir" and "No sir" to strangers, like Buffy and Jody on *Family Affair,* and to keep our clothes clean, because even if we didn't understand what was being said to us, it was important to seem as if we were well brought up. We did this for some time: trying out what we saw and heard on the Magnabox in the world and coming to report successes and failures. And although my mother made use of these bits of information, drilled all of us on them, she found it a very inefficient way to go about learning a language.

She knew that the CRP either offered or connected families with language classes and language tutors. We had neighbors who had books and standing appointments, although every time my mother took the bus to the office indicated on a form or one she had been directed to by someone at the CRP, she would find the class filled, and we would be put on a wait list.

And it was chisme, over the laundry lines stretched in the courtyard of the building when a woman was bragging about all the English she and her husband were getting. My mother says all the woman did when she told her about the lines she had stood in, the wait lists she had been put on, the delays we were suffering without explanation, was point to my mother's arm. And there was nothing that came out of the Magnabox that had prepared us or gave us language for that. The character Diahann Carroll played on *Julia*, was as capable if not more so than Earl J. Wagadorn's mother, and therefore equally as entitled to anything the country had to offer. Nothing showed us that *whiteness* meant *elucidation* and *blackness* could simply symbolize *blackness*.

We all knew that *negro* meant *black* and that we were all, with the exception of my tío Sergio, negro. What was unclear to us was the historical declension of the translation that systematically stripped black bodies of ethnicity as they came to U.S. shores and the entrenched discriminations attached to it. Ten years ago, when my dentist, wanting to "get things clear," asked if I was Cuban or Black, I would have had a readied response. Had he not nearly all of his fingers in my mouth I would have asked him if he was white or born in the United States. But back then, black Cubans only comprised 3 percent of Cuban émigrés, so we were suddenly Black in the U.S., and none of us fully understood the implications of the cognate.

"Which is how come we got the Magnabox," a tía will say, while the sisters nod. We, especially us kids, were going to speak well, sound American, not be embarrassed when we opened our mouths.

The Magnabox was on as a guide. Which may account for my sister's impeccable pre-Parkinson's Katharine Hepburn impersonation. Back then, if anyone said *cool* around my *primo* Enrique, who was no more than three or four at the time, he would automatically parrot, "Cools the burn, eases the pain."

For the two years or so that we were all living together, the set was simply on. It was just the beginning of *Sesame Street*, but that wouldn't have mattered to my mother and her sisters, who insisted education was everywhere, so there were no particular or favored programs with the exception of *I Love Lucy*.

The two daily airings of *I Love Lucy* each evening were the only time that all of us were in front of the box together. Everyone would crowd in, smash together on the Hide-a-Bed, not for Lucy but for

Desiderio Alberto Arnaz y de Acha III. Most of us learned to mispronounce his name like the announcer did—*Arnéz* instead of *Arnaz*—but abuelo only referred to him as Señor Arnaz, because he remembered when Arnaz's father was the mayor of our hometown of Santiago.

It was a strange and vexed realtionship, like the dominos abuelo never let anyone touch or the fighting cocks he insisted he bought but never fought. Because if there was a link between our family and the Arnaz family, who claimed aristocratic blood, other than the place that we had all come from, it was slavery. Though none of my tíos will admit to having watched it now, I believe they watched, like us kids, because at the time Arnaz was the only person on television that sounded like us, sounded like the street we lived on, sounded like most of Habana Pequeña.

If the show comes on in a room now, mother or her sisters say "Mira, it's *I Hate Lucy*." But back then Arnaz was the most romantic figure they could think of.

If anyone had asked us, "Where's home?" we would all say Santiago de Cuba. And Arnaz—as far as my mother and her sisters were concerned, its representative, its guide, and mentor—had mastered the language, succeeded, and survived. And I suppose that they imagined him growing old with a gray-haired Lucy and their two children and all the grandchildren around them, until my mother came home from one of the CRP offices with the information that Arnaz and his wife had divorced long ago.

It had been a woman, not a cubana—"No, never a cubana," a tía will now click—who spoke Spanish and told my mother. Never one to lose an opportunity for more chismes, my mother asked, "*¿Por qué se divorciaron ellos?*"

And whatever it was that she told my mother, it seemed that although *blanco* meant *white*, it translates itself as it passes over the Florida Straits to *Latin*. The woman had gestured to my mother to lean forward as she whispered, "You know how difficult that kind of mixing can be?"

And if you ask my mother and tías about it now, they'll say, "Who knew?" como si es entendido.

H. G. CARRILLO (Santiago de Cuba, Cuba; 1960-) is the author of the novel, *Loosing My Espanish,* and serves as assistant professor in the Department of English at The George Washington University. Carrillo has appeared in many literary journals, including *Kenyon Review, Bomb,* and *Iowa Review.* His awards include a Sage Fellowship, a Newberry Library Research Grant, and two Arthur Lynn Andrews Prizes for Best Fiction.

Wordsranintoeachother

— ESMERALDA SANTIAGO —

Excerpted from *Almost a Woman*

ONE DAY YOLANDA asked me to accompany her to the library. I couldn't, because Mami forbade unplanned stops on the way home from school. "Ask her and we'll go tomorrow. If you bring proof of where you live, you can get a library card," Yolanda suggested, "and you can borrow books. For free," she added when I hesitated.

I'd passed the Bushwick Public Library many times, had wondered about its heavy entrance doors framed by columns, the wide windows that looked down on the neighborhood. Set back from the street behind a patch of dry grass, the red brick structure seemed out of place in a street of rundown apartment buildings and the tall, forbidding projects.

Inside, the ceilings were high, with dangling fixtures over long, brown tables in the center of the room and near the windows. The stacks around the perimeter were crammed with books covered in plastic. I picked up a book from a high shelf, riffled the pages, put it back. I wandered up one aisle, down another. All the books were in English. Frustrated, I found Yolanda, whispered goodbye, and found my way to the front door.

On the way out, I passed the Children's Room, where a librarian read to a group of kids. She read slowly and with expression, and after each page, she turned the book toward us so that we could see the pictures. Each page had only a few words on it, and the illustrations made their meaning clear. If American children could learn English from these books, so could I.

After the reading, I searched the shelves for the illustrated books that contained the words for my new life in Brooklyn. I chose alphabet books, their colorful pages full of cars, dogs, houses, mailmen. I wouldn't admit to the librarian that these elementary books were for me. "For leetle seesters," I said, and she nodded, grinned, and stamped the date due in the back.

I stopped at the library every day after school and at home memorized the words that went with the pictures in the oversized pages. Some concepts were difficult. Snow was shown as huge, multifaceted flakes. Until I saw the real thing, I imagined snow as a curtain of fancy shapes, stiff and flat and possible to capture in my hand.

My sisters and brothers studied the books, too, and we read the words aloud to one another, guessing at the pronunciation.

"Ehr-RAHS-ser," we said for *eraser*. "Keh-NEEF-eh," for *knife*. "Dees" for *this* and "dem" for *them* and "dunt" for *don't*.

In school, I listened for words that sounded like those I'd read the night before. But spoken English, unlike Spanish, wasn't pronounced as written. *Water* became "waddah," *work* was "woik," and wordsranintoeachother in a torrent of confusing sounds that bore no resemblance to the neatly organized letters on the pages of books. In class, I seldom raised my hand, because my accent sent snickers through the classroom the minute I opened my mouth.

Delsa, who had the same problem, suggested that we speak English at home. At first, we broke into giggles whenever we spoke English to each other. Our faces contorted into grimaces, our voices changed as our tongues flapped in our mouths trying to form the awkward sounds. But as the rest of the kids joined us and we practiced between ourselves, it became easier and we didn't laugh as hard. We invented words if we didn't know the translation for what we were trying to say, until we had our own language, neither English nor Spanish, but both in the same sentence, sometimes in the same word.

"Passing me *esa sabanation*," Hector called to Edna, asking her to pass a blanket.

"Stop molestationing me," Edna snapped at Norma when she bothered her.

We watched television with the sound on, despite Tata's complaints that hearing so much English gave her a headache. Slowly, as our vocabularies grew, it became a bond between us, one that separated us from Tata and from Mami, who watched us perplexed, her expression changing from pride to envy to worry.

ESMERALDA SANTIAGO (San Juan, Puerto Rico; 1948-) is a memoirist whose books include *When I Was Puerto Rican*, *The Turkish Lover*, and *Almost a Woman*, which she adapted for PBS Masterpiece Theatre. Her many magazine and newspaper pieces have appeared in, among other outlets, *Sports Illustrated*, *Latina*, *The New York Times*, and *El Nuevo Día*. She is the author of one novel, *America's Dream*, a children's book, *A Doll for Navidades*, and co-editor of two anthologies, *Las Christmas: Favorite Latino Authors Share Their Holiday Memories* and *Las Mamis: Favorite Latino Authors Remember Their Mothers*. Among her honorary doctorates is one from the Universidad de Puerto Rico.

Really

— JOSEFINA LÓPEZ —

WHEN I WAS FIVE years old, I left San Luis Potosí, Mexico, with my mother and little sister and headed to Los Angeles. I remember waiting in a Tijuana bus station for my father to pick us up. I walked around the bus station playing with my little sister. We approached two women in jeans, sitting down and smoking cigarettes. They were speaking in a language I didn't understand. I kept staring at them wanting to know what they were saying. Where were they going? Where were they coming from? I wanted to be like these women who didn't have children and didn't have husbands, they were on their own with an air of confidence and an indescribable quality that made them special. I wondered if it was the language that gave them that confidence or this thing I later learned about: entitlement. I wanted what they had and I wanted to learn English.

The first word I learned was "sorry." I learned it because I thought it sounded like *zorillo*, which means "skunk" in Spanish. So I associated that word with skunks. I remembered it quickly because I figured that if you smelled like a skunk, you should say you are sorry.

I needed to use this word when I was ten years old in second grade. I had told my English as a Second Language teacher that I needed to go to the bathroom, but she didn't think I was serious. She said I would have to wait until recess, two hours away. I lowered my head and sat there wondering what words I could use to convince her to let me go, but they just wouldn't come to me. I fidgeted in my seat trying to hold in my urine. I stared at the clock hoping I could wait the two hours. I held it in as long as I could, but even my prayers to God did not help because I peed all over my pants. I tried to keep it a secret, but when Ms. Garcia, the teacher's assistant, saw me with several paper towels, she discovered my shameful secret.

"I'm sorry," I said to her. Ms. Garcia discreetly went and told the teacher what I did. "Why didn't she tell us she *really* had to go?" my teacher said, a little annoyed but feeling guilty. "I *really* have to go to the bathroom," were the words I wished I had known just an hour earlier. "Really" was the magic word. I realized later that people are accustomed to being lied to, so you have to say "really" to let them know you are telling the truth. I was sent to the nurse, given a new outfit, and sent home. On the way home I admired my new outfit, but I promised myself that I would learn English well enough so this would never happen to me again. Really.

JOSEFINA LÓPEZ (San Luis Potosí, Mexico; 1969-) is the author of the play *Real Women Have Curves* and cowriter of the same-named film, which won the Sundance Film Festival's Audience Award. More than 100 productions of López's plays have been staged in the United States, including *Confessions of a Woman from East L.A.*, *Queen of the Rumba*, and *Lola Goes to Roma*. López teaches screen and playwriting to youth in the Boyle Heights section of Los Angeles.

English Lessons and the Berlitz System

– GERMÁN ARCINIEGAS –

Excerpted from *En el país del rascacielos y las zanahorias*

A SELF-RESPECTING English speaker introduces himself something like this: "I'm Mr. John Nielsen, N-I-E-L-S-E-N." This is due to the fact that in English not only is it assumed that a word will be pronounced one way—not an exact science, by any means—but that it can, and will, be *spelled* a thousand different ways.

At times even spelling a word out may not completely clarify the situation, especially if done over the telephone. If such is the case, the most prudent and customary thing is to say: "Mr. Arciniegas, 'A' as in 'Argentina,' 'R' as in 'Russia,' 'C' as in 'Colombia,' 'I' as in 'Ireland,' 'N' as in 'Nicaragua,' 'I' as in 'Italy,' 'E' as in 'Estonia,' 'G' as in 'Greece,' 'A' as in 'Afghanistan,' 'S' as in 'Somalia.'"

Thus, since this is the language of Shakespeare—the reader will forgive me for not introducing Shakespeare with a word for each of the letters in his name—and since English is such a concise language, a last name can go on indefinitely.

For a case in point, I offer the reader an experience I had yesterday. I was supposed to call Professor Nielsen, pronounced "Neelson" and spelled as I have indicated. I looked up his name in the telephone book and read: "Nielsen (if you do not find the name you are looking for here, see also: Nealson, Neilsen, Neilson, Nilsen, Nilson or Nilsson.") These are the seven different ways of writing "Neelson."

When spelling a last name, you can show special deference to the person you are addressing by choosing letter cues based on some feature you find especially attractive. For example, if the person in question is a farmer, you can say: "Arciniegas, A artichoke, R radish, C cauliflower," etc., and compose a sort of victory garden containing all your favorite vegetables. In addition, some people take advantage of this opportunity to refer to their country of origin–I always say "C as in 'Colombia'"–or to announce its principal products. I remember a Mr. Mejía, a Colombian from the province of Antioquia, who was in this country representing the interests of Antioquian coffee growers. He would always spell out his name by saying, "Medellín, Excelso (the best brand of Antioquian coffee)..."

The possibility of confusion is not limited to the small happenstance of last names. As a fundamental thesis, one can state that all English words are actually hieroglyphs. I published a book entitled, in the Spanish edition, *El Caballero del Dorado*. In this country, it was called *The Knight of El Dorado*. But since in English "knight" and "night" are pronounced exactly the same way, when I talk about my book no one knows if I've written a nocturne or a work on chivalry.

In theater programs, to get out of a bind, instead of spelling night as "night," as it appears in dictionaries, it is written "nite," which is how it sounds. The sound "nite" could just as well denote either "night" or "knight," but the addition of "8 p.m." lets the reader know that we are, in fact, talking about "night." The *gh* removed for theater programs is a letter combination used in English to throw the reader off.

When the above-mentioned version of my book was published, the editors put the following notice on the cover: "Germán Arciniegas (pronounced: Hair-MAHN Ar-seen-YAY-gus)." This notice was indispensable. And if the reader desires any further information on the fate of my last name in this country, I can report that one day the newspaper announced a lecture of mine in the following way: "A lecture on Latin America will be given today by Dr. Arthur Nagus."

One of the chief difficulties of learning English lies in the emission of sounds, which we cannot produce as English speakers do. And when the uninitiated person begins to realize that each letter can be pronounced four or five different ways, he or she often comes dangerously close to fainting. The effort required to produce *r*'s or *s*'s not only causes great fatigue to those of us accustomed to the Spanish language but also causes the painful impression that one is exceedingly dim. I tend to explain it like this to my fellow professors: "I'm not stupid: it's just that I don't know English...." I say this in a confidential tone, which they, in turn, pass on to their colleagues in the same tone. "No, the guy's not stupid; it's just that he doesn't know..."

In my experience, the English language most resembles a type of sickness. It's what one might call, grammatically speaking, a disorder of the tongue. Its symptoms are the sick look on our faces as we speak it, and the fatigue it causes us. When two friends who have traveled in the United States meet again after two or three years, their first conversation is likely to resemble something one might overhear in a clinic: "You know, my English is not in good shape. I've been doing better as far as pronunciation goes, but my 'espeleen' is doing worse and worse." ("Espeleen" is how we of Spanish origin say "spelling.")

The only consolation is to watch foreigners go through the same travail in our country. We all remember that charming anecdote told about Charles V, who, when he arrived in Spain did not speak a word of Spanish and would spend hour after hour just listening, not saying a word. One day an uncouth peasant, seeing him in the plaza with his mouth open, came up to the king and said, "Your Majesty, please close your mouth, because the flies in this town are known to be insolent." After all is said and done, Charles V was not a fool. And if once in a while he did look like an idiot and at other times looked like he was in pain, it was only due to a question of language.

In large American cities, English is learned as if by shorthand. Despite the fact that English now contains more words than Spanish, the man in the street only uses about 80 of these, swallowing half the syllables and deleting all possible letters when it comes to writing. Where you see "U," read "you"; where you see "X," read "kiss"; where you see "nite," night. After just two weeks you have this synthetic language down pat, and you can use it to communicate without difficulty. Sometimes you even have more words than you need. If you go to the grocery store, the "five and dime," or the drug store, you don't have to speak: you just pick up the merchandise, pay, say "thank you," and everything is taken care of.

In this, the American world is the opposite of the Spanish world. Here in the United States, when I go out to buy some ice I say to the ice man: "Fifteen." He understands that I want a 15-cent piece of ice. He answers, "OK," puts the ice in the trunk of the car, and that's it. Sometimes he says, "Nice morning," and I answer, "Beautiful." And with this little friendly touch the transaction is as perfectly complete as a work of art.

In Spain this kind of thing unfolds in a completely different way. In a similar situation I would say to the ice man, "Please be so kind as to sell me 15 cents' worth of ice." His answer would be immediately forthcoming: "How is your mother? Wasn't that bullfight yesterday a disaster?! Can you imagine anything worse?..." etc. In other words, in Spain the ice would come as a kind of afterthought, and meanwhile the foreigner would be treated to sumptuous instruction in the Spanish language.

The Berlitz system is based on the American experience of life. It is a method for learning conversational English. Neither grammar nor vocabulary have anything to do with it. The zenith of understanding reached by the student is crystallized in the following sentence, which I heard when I was learning languages at the Berlitz school and which I have never been able to forget: "The green book is bigger than the red book that is on the table."

Using the Berlitz system, as earnestly learned in an American Berlitz school, you can go to a store and tell the salesperson: "My head is bigger than the black hat in the window." With this, the clerk will realize that you want a bigger hat, and that you want to buy a hat. But even in this case, it turns out that the system is too effusive. The buyer has in fact used 10 or 12 words too many in this sentence, because what one usually does is say, "Hat," put on the hat, and pay.

Perhaps it is for this reason that the thousands of words recorded in English dictionaries are useless.

GERMÁN ARCINIEGAS (Bogotá, Colombia; 1900–1999) was a widely traveled author, historian, journalist, educator, and diplomat. His numerous books, which include *Why America? 500 Years of a Name–The Life and Times of Amerigo Vespucci* and *Latin American: A Cultural History,* address the nature of society and power in the Americas.

Soda and Nylons— Learning English Was No Pignic

— GUILLERMO LINARES —

LEARNING ENGLISH HAS BEEN a lengthy process for me. My first episode with the language came during the summer of 1965 in Santo Domingo, the capital of the Dominican Republic. I was 14 years old and it was the first time three of my brothers and sisters and I were in a bustling city far away from our farm in rural Cabrera.

Our parents were in New York. They had finally received their Green Cards and immediately petitioned for four of the seven children they left behind. In Santo Domingo, we would wait a half a year for our flight to New York. We stayed at the home of a family friend in a rough neighborhood called Villa Juana.

Santo Domingo was under U.S. military occupation at the time, and we were forbidden to wander the streets. Machine gun fire accompanied our breakfast and lunch and shattered the evenings. Indoors and bored, one day I asked one of the young men living in the house how to say *adios* in English. "Goodbye," he responded. Minutes later, I saw a U.S. military Jeep passing the front of the house and I cried out to the soldiers the word I had just learned, waving to them in a gesture of friendship as they drove by. The young man who had taught me the word looked at me with disbelief. He rushed out of the house to catch up with the passing Jeep and started shouting, "YANKEES, GO HOME! YANKEES, GO HOME!" He wanted to make sure that the soldiers understood that they were rejected, that they were part of an invading force. I did not fully comprehend the context of the military invasion until my college years, when I read about U.S.-Dominican history. Then, I understood his anger.

We were so excited to finally join our parents at a six-story apartment building in the East Tremont section of the Bronx. My first day there, my mother sent me on an errand. She gave me a dollar and asked me to buy a "soda" at the neighborhood bodega.

When I entered the store, I began to look around and the owner asked me in Spanish what he could help me with. I told him and he pointed to a refrigerator full of soft drinks. I simply stared at the bottles. He asked again, and I told him I was looking for something in a box, not in a bottle, and that it was not cold. I told him it was *bicarbonato de soda*. He led me to an aisle where he dusted off a box and handed it to me.

When I came home with the box, my mother was surprised and told me that that was not what she wanted. She had forgotten that we use the word *refrescos* for sodas in the Dominican Republic. I went back to the store, embarrassed to exchange the baking soda, and the owner admitted that he had been surprised by my request.

The same week that I arrived, my mother successfully lobbied the owner of the grocery store, Don Rafael, to hire me. One day he had to run an errand and left me in charge. A lady came in who looked Latina, and I expected familiar words. "Can I have a pair of stockings?" she asked in English. I had no idea what she was talking about and I looked at her with a big question mark on my face. "Do you have stockings?" I remained silent. The third time she said it, she pointed to the wall behind me to help me find whatever she was in search of. I turned and saw shelves and racks of just about anything and everything, and I began pointing at different things, hoping to match something with whatever she wanted. I pointed to a can of sardines, to boxes of cake flour, then to a sack of rice. She shook her head and huffed. "Nylons—nylons—nylons," she demanded. I breathed a sigh of relief. I knew what nylon was.

It was the line I used to go fishing in my hometown. I looked frantically all over the wall to find the fishing line, but it was nowhere. Steam seemed to lift out of her head. Just then Don Rafael walked in and plucked a pair of stockings from a rack.

I eventually left my job at the bodega after a guy entered with a double-barrel shotgun. I didn't need any translation.

I had worked for more than a year in the bodega and was learning English little by little, enough to move on to a neighborhood supermarket. One afternoon there, a customer dropped a bunch of glass bottles in one of the aisles. The assistant manager summoned me to the scene and asked me to run to the back room and get some "sawdust." I stood still for a moment, not understanding. Before I could say anything, he screamed at me to go and hurry back. I could not understand why he was asking for "sodas" when something was broken on the floor. But I ran back and picked up a large box of Coca-Colas and returned with the heavy box. When he saw me turn into the aisle with the box, he put his hands on his head and screamed, "What the hell are you doing?" He ordered me to leave the box and get the sawdust. I followed another clerk with the same task to the back, and finally it all made sense.

During my third year of high school, a cousin of mine traveled from Venezuela to finish school in New York and learn English. I had just started working in another supermarket and managed to get him a job.

On his first day at the supermarket, we worked at opposite ends of an aisle, sticking prices on cans. Most of the customers in the store only spoke English, so when he was approached the first time for assistance, he sent the person to me. By then, I had a grasp of English from practice at work and school.

My cousin referred another customer to me. Then a lady approached him and in a loud voice asked, "Do you have Spic and Span?" He matched her loudness. "Yes, Yes, I speak Spanish! I speak Spanish!" The lady could not make sense of his response and wasn't sure whether he was making fun of her. I explained that he didn't know English and offered to help her find Spic and Span, a product to clean floors.

During my first semester in college, I took an English writing class. On the first day of class, the teacher asked each student to write an essay about a summer experience. I decided to write about a family picnic in Cabrera. When the teacher asked for volunteers to share their stories, I was one of the few who jumped at the chance. He asked all of the volunteers to write the title of their story on the board. As I wrote mine, I heard giggling and whispers behind me. The teacher said there was an error with the one of the words I had written. I took another look but could not find a mistake in my title, which read: "My Experience with a Pignic in the Dominican Republic." The teacher and students said that I had misspelled the word *picnic*. But I was like one of the old mules in Cabrera. I told them that when we had picnics, or *pasadías* in my hometown, my family always roasted a pig.

Reading textbooks in college, then teaching fifth- and six-graders in elementary school, and more than 15 years of volunteer work teaching English as a Second Language, high school equivalency, and literacy to adults—all this lay the foundation for the English I speak today.

GUILLERMO LINARES (Cabrera, Dominican Republic; 1951-) has been a cab driver, schoolteacher, and member of the New York City Council, to which he was elected in 1991. A graduate of City College of New York and Columbia Teachers College, in 2004 he was appointed Commissioner of the New York City Mayor's Office of Immigrant Affairs.

Good Food and a Good Fastball Taught Me English

– JUAN MARICHAL –

THE LANGUAGE BARRIER and the unfamiliar surroundings of the United States made me feel strange and uncomfortable when I first reported to the Giants' big minor league training camp in the late winter of 1958. The Giants liked to start their pitchers far down and let them set their own pace for advancement, and it was not easy for a Spanish-speaking player to catch on right away.

So I became a pitcher for the Michigan City, Mississippi, team. Perhaps the toughest part of my life in organized baseball was made easy for me by Buddy Kerr, the manager, because for a Latin American who spoke no English, to travel through the American South was not exactly the most wonderful opportunity in the world.

Our team traveled 300 hundred miles by bus from Sanford, Mississippi, to Michigan City, and as long as we were in the South, there were no restaurants that would serve the Negroes or Dominicans or Puerto Ricans on the team. We would stay on the bus, and Kerr himself would go inside and bring us our food.

For the 1959 season I was moved up to Springfield, Massachusetts, of the Eastern League, and in 1960, I made it to the Tacoma, Washington, triple-A team, under manager Red Davis.

I was in Tacoma for only half a season. San Francisco Giants' manager Tom Sheehan called me up to the "Big Show." I was 21 years old at the time, and the only big league baseball I had ever seen was on television when I was playing in Mississippi.

Felipe Alou from the Dominican Republic and Orlando Cepeda from Puerto Rico were already playing with the San Francisco club. Within a year we would be joined by Felipe's brother Matty, José Pagán, and Manny Mota. I knew the Alous from home, so meeting up with Felipe was quite a relief. Cepeda and I became instant friends, even roommates, for that matter. The presence of Felipe was especially fortunate for me when I first joined the Giants, because he lived next door to a wonderful woman named Blanche Johnson, and she and her husband took me in as a boarder. When Matty Alou came up from Tacoma, they took him in, too. The Johnsons were die-hard Giants fans and were quite pleased to have a couple of players under their roof. Their house was small, a two-bedroom/one-bath, but certainly much better living quarters than those I may have had in the Dominican or the minors. Blanche taught us English, and how to live in the United States, and in turn we taught her how to cook *arroz con pollo* and other Dominican dishes.

One of her successful techniques was to send us to the grocery store with the shopping list. The first couple of times I was gone for hours, but since the list rarely varied, shopping became easier each trip. Also, every morning before heading to the ballpark, she would give us English lessons by using elementary flash cards. We would say the name of the item in Spanish and she would repeat it for us in English. Gradually, we became "Americanized," and the food became a magnificent blending of our dishes and those of Mama, as we insisted on calling her. Although I preferred steak for dinner, Mama Johnson had become quite fond of dishes like rice and beans and fed it to us frequently. I would ask her for more "American dishes" but she insisted that the best way to learn English was to learn it while feeling at home. Mama insisted we speak only English in her presence, and this certainly helped speed up the process.

I wasn't that fluent in English yet, in any event. During those first couple of years, catcher Hobie Landrith and I would communicate according to the opposing team's hitters' numbers on their backs because I would recognize those faster than I would their names. My other teammates were also helpful, for my interest in learning the language was apparent to them. They would laugh at my mistakes, but told me not to give up, that I would eventually get there.

I will never forget spring training 1962. I arrived in Phoenix a married man accompanied by Alma Rosa, my young and beautiful bride whom I had met back home through the Alous. Alma knew no English at the time, so I showed off my second language. Alma seemed quite impressed, unaware of the mistakes I may have made while speaking.

I am a competitive person by nature and this certainly influenced my degree of success at the game of baseball. It also influenced my desire to learn English and adapt to living in the United States. Having joined the Dominican Air Force, where I played baseball, served as a wonderful foundation for discipline not only in sports but in life overall. Discipline was what encouraged me to learn the language to better myself as an athlete and as a foreigner. Everyday— game-days and off-days—I would read everything that fell into my hands. I would do homework with my children, not necessarily to help them out but to put myself through English-speaking grade school. Slowly but surely, my English improved to the point where I can now say with confidence that I am truly bilingual.

JUAN MARICHAL (Laguna Verde, Dominican Republic; 1937-) pitched major league baseball for 16 years, almost all of those with the San Francisco Giants. His overall record was 243 victories and 142 losses, giving up an average of 2.89 earned runs per game. Among the statistics that earned Marichal induction into the National Baseball Hall of Fame in 1983 were his 2,303 career strikeouts and his six seasons winning 20 or more games. In retirement, he has served as his country's Minister of Sports and Physical Education. He is the author of *A Pitcher's Story*.

Breaking Down the Glass Walls of Language

— ARIEL DORFMAN —

THAT'S WHAT I'D LOVE to be able to remember: the moment when it happened. Or at least remember the days, the weeks, the way in which English crept into my brain, flooded into my life, hit me like lightning.

It's a memory denied to me, accessible only through others, *através de otros*, through the stories my parents told me later, when I was puzzling about my conversion from Spanish to English, when I searched out *los orígenes* of my love affair with the language of Shakespeare and Ogden Nash, Superman, and, well, Richard Nixon as well.

This I do know: it was February 1945 and snow was falling in New York when I arrived there, a toddler of two and a half, whose skin must still have recollected the sweltering Buenos Aires where he had been born, the Buenos Aires of Borges and Perón that he had only just left behind. Maybe that child was lodging a protest against the first of his many exiles or maybe the reasons were less metaphorical and a tad more medical. Whatever the explanation, the cold and undeniable fact is that I came down with pneumonia.

Recently, as part of a film based on my life, I managed to track down the hospital where I spent those three decisive weeks when I learned English. It was Mount Sinai, way up on Fifth Avenue in front of Central Park, and the woman who had been the head nurse for pediatrics in the 1940s was still volunteering there, though now well into her 90s. She showed me photos of the children's ward, where young patients with my sort of contagious disease were secluded inside large glass-partitioned cubicles, isolated from any outside visitors, only in contact with doctors and nurses and other sick boys and girls. Today they would not segregate that infant. And today he would undoubtedly be surrounded by an array of Hispanics, Latinos, Nuyoricans, whatever you want to call them, today *mi idioma materno*, my mother tongue, Spanish, would be floating around everywhere. Indeed, today Anglo-speaking kids might emerge from that experience with a smattering of *castellano*, knowing how to say *hola* and *gracias* and *quiero más*. But back then it was English and only English wherever I turned, an immersion course *a la fuerza*. *Mi papá y mamá* were allowed to visit only once a week and then, always, they have told me, from the distance, from behind that glass wall watching their son cry and reach out for them. And then what did I do, what else could I do after they had mouthed an adios I was unable to hear, what alternative did I have but to survive, adapt and survive—motivated by the same needs that pressed humans to chance on language as they roamed the plains of Africa so many hundreds of thousands of years ago.

And that's how I learned this language in which I now write these words. Out of sheer necessity. I learned the vocabulary of sustenance and sleep and love from those who healed my lungs and fed me. From those who coddled me at night and played with me in the morning. Almost as if I had to give birth to myself in that hospital ward, midwife myself into a second language.

I must have felt betrayed by my Spanish syllables, by Cervantes and Darío and Sor Juana, even if I had no idea at that point that such future mentors of my literary tongue were awaiting me. And I must have felt abandoned by my parents, *pobrecitos*, my parents who loved me *más que el sol*. Oh, I must have planned my petty revenge.

Because I am told that when I left that hospital after that three-week stay, not only was my pneumonia gone. So was my Spanish.

I refused to answer when spoken to in the language into whose waters I had gently been cast, been swimming through, since my inaugural breaths on this Earth. "I don't understand," my mother says that I said, perhaps the first words she ever heard me pronounce in the language in which she would have to speak to me during the next ten years. Except that she never lost her accent, and I never had one, still can "pass" for American.

My forced conversion—like so many captives throughout history—is, of course, only part of the story. English did not come exclusively as a conqueror, merely as a threat. It was awaiting me in the years ahead and in the streets outside. It was the funnies on Sunday in the *New York Herald Tribune*. It was the legend of Babe Ruth's magical sixty home runs. It was the "Teddy Bears' Picnic." It was kindergarten's tales of wonder and two-plus-two-equals-four. And someday it would be William Faulkner and John Wayne, William Blake and Joan Baez, *The Sands of Iwo Jima* and "The Times They Are a-Changin'," and, of course, Ella Fitzgerald.

Later I would return to Latin America, fall in love once more with *el idioma de mi nacimiento*, even come, in a moment of extreme folly, to repudiate English because of its connections to the U.S. Empire that was subjugating *la América de Martí*—only to find myself buffeted by yet another exile, *décadas más tarde*, find myself once again back in the States, back in the land which first gave me the gift of its language.

Except that now, in this land which I have made my own, I am not alone in the quest to make that tongue my own. That initial experience of mine is being repeated and resurrected by millions of other Latino voices, all of us part of a gigantic migratory wave which will transform the language that rushed to my rescue during those dark days of 1945, all of us simply trying to survive. Here I am, more than half a century later, still seduced by those words I first heard, even if I can't remember them, the day I stumbled into that hospital ward and realized that my mouth and tongue and teeth would save me, could save me, from starvation and loneliness.

ARIEL DORFMAN (Buenos Aires, Argentina; 1942-) is the author of numerous works, including *Heading South, Looking North: A Bilingual Journey, The Last Song of Manuel Sendero, Mascara, The Nanny and the Iceberg,* and *Exorcising Terror: The Incredible Ongoing Trial of General Augusto Pinochet.* His works as a playwright and screenwriter include *Death and the Maiden,* and he has been active with a wide range of international organizations such as UNESCO and the French Académie Universelle de Cultures. He is a fellow of the American Academy of Arts and Sciences and teaches at Duke University.

How I Learned
English...or Did I?

— MAYRA MONTERO —

AS A CHILD, during the first years of the Cuban Revolution, I took
Russian classes in school. If by chance I ran into a Soviet citizen
in the street, generally pasty-white provincial types wearing san-
dals over black socks (all of which left us bursting with laughter),
I would try to practice the phrases I had learned. My father would
look at me sadly, "You should be studying English..."

In addition to Russian, which I later forgot almost entirely, I enrolled
in Chinese classes—Pekinese, as they called it then—being offered near
my house, in the venerable Society for Chinese-Cuban Friendship.
The professor, whose name was Cecil Pan, used to say that my calligraphy was perfect, and would show my work as an example to the
rest of the students: girls and boys with Asian features, but Cuban
to their marrow, who, because they were children or grandchildren
of immigrants and residents of Havana's crowded Chinatown, were
obligated by their parents to take classes at the Society. None of them
were the least interested in learning the language of their ancestors. I
was. I would immerse myself in my homework. When my father saw
me writing those characters on rice paper, he would warn me warily,
"You should be learning something else..."

One fine day he brought home an English teacher. He was an older
man, hailing from Trinidad and Tobago. He had a thick voice and
an air like Louis Armstrong. He had come to teach me, dressed in a
jacket and tie, roasting in the July heat. We sat at a table on the patio,
and he took lessons out of his briefcase. The lessons had a colonial,
Victorian air, quite anachronistic for the Communist effervescence

in which we lived. I remember one afternoon he made me practice something rather snobbish regarding the correct manner of drinking five o'clock tea. The elderly teacher would wipe off his sweat with a soiled handkerchief. Watching him, I would also sweat—and be intensely bored. At that time, Cuban children and adolescents listened to music that came mostly from Mexico and Spain. Because of this, we did not have the incentive that teenagers in other countries have had, who, listening to rock in English and now rap in English, end up learning from the pure temptation of understanding what their favorite singers were saying.

The old man would torment me for an hour, then would charge for the class and leave, walking away slowly due to his age and girth. I would return to my Chinese and my Russian, two languages that would do nothing for me in the future but that filled my childhood dreams with beautiful Cyrillic pen strokes and the no less beautiful Eastern figures.

Once outside of Cuba, the moment I reached Puerto Rico, I realized that my father had been right. Without knowing English, not only would I not get a good job but I would be lost in this world and before God. I went through I-don't-know-how-many academies that promised me a complete knowledge of the language in three months. Maybe these programs worked for others, but they certainly didn't work for me. When it came time to put my knowledge to practice, I would start to stutter. I would forget the auxiliary verbs, mix up the past tenses, and the future would stick in my throat. Never was it better said: without fluency there is no future. I would torture myself thinking of everything I had said wrong, and of the greatest of ironies of the fact that, although my brain knew what I wanted to say, my tongue would freeze. It still freezes.

I turned to love. I held trysts with people who did not speak a word of Spanish. They spoke English, and I came to hope that sign language, those little romantic gestures, and lust—the mother of all understanding—would create the ideal setting and release me.

I began to think that there was a "click" in my brain closed to English syntax, an ancient trauma from my childhood that the fat old teacher from Trinidad and Tobago had inflicted on me.

Years later, when I started traveling to the United States on publicity tours to promote my novels, the suffering sharpened to the point where I began to wonder if it would not be more convenient to acquire a new identity as a mute writer. Are there not authors who are blind, deaf, paranoid, or slightly lame? Could a line not be added to my biography declaring that the author, born in Havana, had lost her vocal cords at the age of three? As a mute, nobody could expect me to speak in any language. They could ask me questions, yes, and I could write the answers on a chalkboard, in decent English, since I can write it better now. But the idea did not take hold, considering how difficult it would be for me to proclaim myself mute in my own language, the Spanish that I adore and never tire of speaking.

I confess that, although I now manage to communicate whenever I wish, I have the feeling that I never learned English. I have learned to fight against the panic, against the grave fear, and, above all, against the feeling of inferiority that grips me each time I must speak English in public or read fragments of my own books in translation. The years have brought with them resignation, which is another way of learning. I now know that I will never speak English like I want to. But sometimes I murmur the language between dreams; I wake up pronouncing a phrase that I heard in a movie—usually from Bette Davis—or that I read in a book. This is the mystery of memory without prejudice—the part of one's soul that, in any language, makes itself listen.

MAYRA MONTERO (Havana, Cuba; 1952-) is a Sunday columnist for the San Juan daily *El Nuevo Día*. Montero has worked as a sports writer, international journalist, and editorialist. More than a half-dozen of her novels have appeared in English, including *In the Palm of Darkness*, *The Messenger*, and, most recently, *Dancing to Almendra*.

Nothing Seemed Unreachable after Traveling through Europe in a Used Red Lada

– ALEJANDRO NECOCHEA –

WHEN I WAS FIVE years old in Lima, Peru, my father taught me how to say, "How are you?" It was my first exposure to English. All I could think of was how those three syllables sounded like the Spanish word for "jaguar" plus the word "you." I pictured a man, maybe an explorer, greeting a jaguar.

My parents, both physicians, saw the importance of my brother Raúl and me learning a second language from a young age, so they enrolled us in English lessons every year for as long as I can remember. I was too young and distractible to understand the value of learning a new language, and I repeated some of the basic levels an embarrassing number of times. Raúl, 11 months my senior, conquered each level without difficulty. By the time I was ten, he was already several levels above me. It stung that he had gotten so far ahead, so I got my act together.

Two years later, my mother had the opportunity to spend a year in the United Kingdom training in obstetrics and gynecology. This was a chance for Raúl and me to fully immerse ourselves in the

English language and culture. We had traveled to the Unites States as tourists before, but this would be different. My dad, Raúl, and I joined my mom in Newcastle, and soon my brother and I were enrolled in Heworth Grange Comprehensive School with dozens of students whose only exposure to Latin America was Mirandinha, a Brazilian soccer player for Newcastle United.

Those four months in school were hard. I was shy and didn't really make any friends, and the days were punctuated by awkward interactions. Geography was one of my favorite subjects back home, but suddenly I could barely recognize the names of most places. In English class, I struggled for days to write a poem assigned for homework–it was terrible despite my efforts. I still remember my teacher cringing as she read it. At least in home economics there was little talking–until they asked me what kinds of things people ate in Peru. Since my English wasn't good enough to explain *ceviche*, *ají de gallina*, or *lomo saltado*, I simply said that some people ate guinea pig. At that moment (I should have known from my peers' expressions), I became one of the most unpopular kids in my class.

Toward the end of our stay in the UK, my family and I took a trip around Europe for a month in a used red Lada we had bought in England. We traveled from Britain to Yugoslavia and back, visiting all the countries in between. We communicated in English, Spanish, and my mom's French, or a combination of the three, and somehow managed to make ourselves understood. We saw remarkable places and met fascinating people. I quickly forgot about the tough times in Heworth Grange. Instead, I saw a world of opportunities ahead. Nothing seemed unreachable.

When we returned to Peru, language school became much easier, and it felt good to do well in class. I passed the British Proficiency exam, and later the test for Teaching of English as a Foreign Language. During high school, Raúl and I moved on to French. At that point I was into body-boarding. Surfer kids in Peru tended to listen to reggae, so I kept up with my English by listening to Bob Marley. I spent hours deciphering the lyrics to his songs—Jamaican slang and Rastafarian lingo all the more challenging in the pre-Internet era.

After I finished high school, my father was hired to work in the United States and he proposed that I go with him to attend college there. Because I didn't go to an American high school in Peru, the college application process proved cumbersome, requiring translations, official letters, and a lot of red tape. While I applied and waited for a decision, I took an extra year of high school at Boston College High. MTV was my most reliable tutor in American customs, culture, and slang; every day I learned what was "cool" from shows like *The Real World* or *Beavis & Butthead*.

I had a better working knowledge of English in New England than in Olde England. In fact, English as a Second Language courses became boring, and I understood enough to do well in classes like calculus and history. Since I felt I had spent my share of hours in religion classes growing up in Peru, early in the year I asked the principal to waive the religion requirement so I could enroll in something else. Only advanced placement (AP) classes were available, and he insisted that those were reserved for students who had done well in those subjects previously. I really didn't want to go back to religion class, so after reviewing the list of courses available, I asked the principal to give me a chance at AP biology. After shaking his head, he reluctantly agreed.

Frankly, I had barely taken biology in Peru and was far more interested in economics than biology, but the biology teacher, Mr. Toto, was engaging and inspiring. Though on a few occasions I talked about deoxyribonucleic acid as "ADN" (the Spanish acronym, instead of DNA, the English one), learning new biology terms wasn't too difficult overall. Many of the words, like *phagocytosis, arthropod*, or *epidermis*, had Greek roots and meant the same in Spanish, or I could guess the meaning from dissecting the etymology of words I knew in Spanish. Soon biology became my favorite time of day, and at the end of the year I received the AP biology award. After graduation, I started college and decided to major in biology, which eventually led to my interest in medicine.

Looking back, learning English was one of the most important aspects of my education. My attitude toward learning English changed as I grew up and matured. But also, who I am was in many ways shaped by my experiences learning English. Once I became truly bilingual I was able to use my skills to help others overcome the language barrier, first as a student, by working as an interpreter in different hospitals of Boston, and later on as a doctor, by being able to communicate with my Spanish-speaking patients and their families. Being bilingual has also allowed me to carry out research in Latin America, and largely because of those experiences, helped me shape my interest in improving the quality of health care in underserved populations. Knowing English opened doors that led me to new discoveries and interests, and to explore my potential. It allowed me to attend college and medical school and to meet amazing people in the United States and other countries. Though I initially saw it as an annoyance that my parents put me through, I eventually realized how powerful it was to be able to share my ideas and opinions with people from around the world, and how privileged I was to be able to understand theirs.

ALEJANDRO NECOCHEA (Lima, Peru; 1976-), an internal medicine resident at the University of Pennsylvania, has researched hepatitis among HIV patients in the Dominican Republic and tuberculosis in a Lima shantytown. At Yale University School of Medicine he organized to increase minority participation in the health professions, and captained the med school soccer team. He has co-presented papers dealing with diabetes, high altitude, and epilepsy.

Doris Day, John Kennedy, and Me

— TERESA MÉNDEZ-FAITH —

WHEN I THINK BACK to my earliest memories of at what moment, how, and why I wanted to learn English, two incidents from my childhood and early youth come vividly to mind. The first is likely related to what I had seen in the movies, and the second—still fresh in my mind despite the passage of time—from the early 1960s when John Kennedy was on the political scene in the United States.

As my mother tells it, I was seven or eight years old when some-one asked me, surely as a joke, when and who I would marry. I immediately blurted out, "I'll marry when I'm older and it will be with a 'Yankee,' not a Paraguayan." And I well remember the follow-up question: "Why a 'Yankee' and not a Paraguayan?" Because, I explained, North American men help their wives in the kitchen, they wash the dishes and take care of the children. Unlike Paraguayan men, I said, they don't think those jobs are only for women.

Where in the world did those ideas come from? I had not yet traveled outside my country! I am sure they came from the movies, in particular the two or three Doris Day movies I must have seen, where everyone got along well and lived comfortably without any financial problems whatsoever: the perfect world of my dreams.

More vivid still are my memories of the early 1960s, when I was barely an adolescent and living in Montevideo, Uruguay. My father had arrived there in 1956 as a political exile from the dictatorship of Alfredo Stroessner and my mother and we six children followed him three years later.

I went to high school in Montevideo, and the old saying, "Behind every cloud is a silver lining," applied to me. My father's exile gave my siblings and me access to Uruguay's primary and secondary educational programs, one of the best in South America at that time.

High school students were required to study two languages: four years of English and two years of French. So began my formal English education; I was 13 years old and in my first year of high school. As I recall, the classes were very large (40 to 50 students and more) and students barely had the opportunity to speak the language. We only wrote and translated. As a result, we developed a strong vocabulary and reading skills, but without oral practice, our ability to speak English was extremely weak. From time to time, we had to memorize something to recite, if there was time and the teacher called on us. I remember one assignment I liked very much—the teacher, I believe in my senior year, asked us to memorize four verses of a poem of our choosing in English, and then to translate it into Spanish. I had read that John F. Kennedy's favorite poet was Robert Frost, whose work he often cited. At the time, I was a great Kennedy admirer, so I decided to translate his favorite lines. After reading several Frost poems, and discovering in the process that I liked his poetry, I came upon the poem "Stopping by Woods on a Snowy Evening," whose final lines I associated with Kennedy. "The woods are lovely, dark, and deep / But I have promises to keep, / And miles to go before I sleep, / And miles to go before I sleep."

I translated the lines, with the help of a dictionary, and the following day I delivered the page to my teacher. "Robert Frost...?" she said. "He is my favorite poet! Read the verses you chose and let's see what the class thinks about what the poet is saying." I did what she said, and although I was extremely nervous and red in the face, the teacher complimented my pronunciation and asked if I had been studying English elsewhere on the side. I said no, but that I would like to continue studying so I could speak and communicate with people in English.

She recommended that I study at the Alianza Cultural Uruguay-Estados Unidos and a few months later, in March 1963, I enrolled there.

While I was still in high school, and a few months after having begun my English studies at the Alianza, I heard about a contest for scholarships to study in the United States. It was the "Youth for Understanding" program, available to Uruguayan youth under 17 who were proficient enough in English to live with an American family and attend an American high school as a senior. I scored the highest on the contest's written exam, and even though I was not Uruguayan and my family could not afford the round-trip airfare to the United States, they awarded me the scholarship. My travel, they explained, would be covered by Fulbright funds. As Isabel Allende might say, this was my destiny.

In a group of 50 young scholars from Uruguay sent to spend their senior year 1963–64 studying in the United States, there were forty-nine Uruguayans and one Paraguayan.

When I won the scholarship in the middle of 1963, I never would have guessed that, before I could achieve one of my greatest dreams, to travel to the United States, the great John F. Kennedy would already be dead. But that is how it happened, and the pain of that recent American tragedy clouded my personal joy as I arrived in the country on December 31, 1963, first in New York and hours later in Michigan, where my American family awaited me.

My informal training in English began the moment I landed in New York, and I quickly realized that my years of formal studies had not prepared me to understand the spoken language. My first linguistic shock was delivered at U.S. Immigration, when agents at the airport questioned me in a routine manner—asking me my name, country of origin, why I was visiting, and for how long. I didn't understand a word. To me, they spoke too quickly, they ate their syllables, and they didn't pronounce the words in the way to which I was accustomed. A phrase such as "What is your name?" ran together and sounded like "Whatchorname?" I understood nothing and as I became more and more anxious, tears came flooding from my eyes. "Please repeat your questions slowly," I pleaded, and so they did. The agents had to repeat each question several times, but finally they finished their interrogation and I entered the United States!

It was like an immersion program; English surrounded me on all sides. At first I was frightened that I would be so lost in class that they would send me back to Montevideo. How that would embarrass and disappoint my family and those who had done all they could to make this trip possible. That was the only thing on my mind during the entire flight from New York to Detroit, and from there on the bus to Ann Arbor. Luckily, my doubts and anguish vanished almost as soon as we arrived, when Kenny and Sherry, my "American siblings," and "Mom" and "Dad" Hannon came running and embraced me warmly. It was here that I also had what I could describe as my first cultural shock. I not only returned the embraces, but also gave two kisses (one on each cheek) to each family member. Although they said nothing at the time, I discovered afterwards—because Sherry told me—that people are not accustomed to such an effusive welcome in this country. She even said that kisses between women could be misinterpreted and so it was better not to do it. I followed her advice from that moment on.

For seven months, I lived with the Hannons in Mt. Morris, a small Michigan town just north of Flint, and attended Saint Mary's High School. I did well in my courses, made a number of friends, and met Ray, a junior college student who a few years later would travel to Montevideo to marry me (thus fulfilling my declaration that I would marry a Yankee). I graduated with the seniors of my high school, traveled and had great experiences, and, in particular, improved my English immeasurably. In seven months, I learned more than I had in five years of formal English classes. Nonetheless, now that I've been a Spanish professor for many years, I am sure those five years of formal studies gave me the foundation I needed to take full advantage of the seven months of linguistic immersion. I also was fortunate to be placed with a monolingual family. Neither my American "siblings" nor "parents" spoke a word of Spanish, only English.

Upon my return to Montevideo, I resumed English classes at the Alianza, now with a view to earn my certificate in TESL (Teacher of English as a Second Language), which I received at the end of 1966. I also pursued studies at the Facultad de Ciencias Económicas. And at the end of 1967 I married the American who won my heart during my time in Michigan, and my studies in Uruguay were cut short. Nonetheless, when I returned to the United States in 1968, I continued to practice my English, now married and with the best language immersion program of all: constant practice inside and outside the house!

While I learned English live and direct 100 percent of the time, I also studied at the University of Michigan and, now with a young son at home, I pursued my degrees in Spanish—undergraduate, master's, and finally a doctorate in 1979. Those degrees have allowed me to teach Spanish and Latin American literature at Saint Anselm College in New Hampshire for more than 20 years.

After this long tour through significant moments in my English education, I can explain how I learned English in eight simple words: studying and living the language, formally and informally. In my case, something that caused much pain and suffering in my family, the political exile of my father to Uruguay, was also of benefit to me. If it hadn't been for that, I would not have started studying English at age 13 or won a scholarship to the United States while still a teenager. I would not have met the man who became my husband or have come to live and study in this country and thus benefit from the best English program that one could ask for: total immersion in the language and culture of those two inspiring heroes of my youth—Doris Day and John Kennedy.

From her office in the Spanish Department at Saint Anselm College in New Hampshire, **TERESA MÉNDEZ-FAITH** (Asunción, Paraguay; 1945-) has labored to promote the languages, literature, and culture of her native country and the rest of Latin America. She does this through books, instructional material, theater, and a Web page that leads to music, recipes, and Guarani language and culture. Her most recent book is *Antología de la literatura paraguaya*.

Advantages of the Civilized World

– OSCAR HIJUELOS –

Excerpted from *Conversations with Ilan Stavans*

I SPOKE SPANISH until I was four years old when I still lived in Holguín, Cuba. It was then that I became ill with nephrosis. I was sick and I was taken to the United States to a hospital in Connecticut. I was hospitalized for a year. I entered the hospital speaking Spanish and left it speaking English. The nurse that took care of me was a strong and strict Protestant. I complained, asked her for medicine, an aspirin. She paid no attention to me. I would scream and cry…"Please help me!" When I finally made the same supplication in English, she heeded my request. It was with her that I learned English.

That's how I remember my linguistic transition, although truth be told, I doubt that the nurse ever existed and that that memory is real. It is possible that my imagination simply went rampant. I do know, though, I only spoke to my parents in English, and they would answer me in Spanish. I've an older brother who is an artist, who speaks a fluent Spanish even though he often makes mistakes. I've lost mine. I can repeat some curse words and some romantic lines—nothing more.

That year, my family crumbled. It was terrible. Upon returning home we were all strangers. Even still, I think my parents were still in awe of the fact that I had survived my illness through a simple switch to the American universe. From then on, they saw me as being higher up the social ladder. It was their understanding that I had the advantages of the civilized world at my feet.

Although born in the States, **OSCAR HIJUELOS** (New York, New York; 1951-) went to Cuba with his Cuban parents at a very young age. The family returned to the United States when he was four. He is best known for *The Mambo Kings Play Songs of Love*, awarded the Pulitzer Prize for Fiction (1990). His other novels include *The Fourteen Sisters of Emilio Montez O'Brien*, *A Simple Habana Melody*, and *Empress of the Splendid Season*. He has also coedited two volumes of poetry.

El Dobbing and My English

— IGNACIO PADILLA —

LATIN AMERICA IS FAR from being a strictly bilingual continent, as a good part of Africa or India might be today. With some exceptions, children here grow up speaking Spanish or Portuguese, while English is a matter of formal education. The vast majority of Latin Americans of my generation would say that we learned English for survival, by chance, and in the schoolroom. These three statements would be true but inconclusive. Thinking it through, a good deal of my education in this so curious, so rebellious, and so unsystematic a language took place through simple infection, from being constantly exposed to its pathological germs. I'm referring not only to music and computer talk but specifically to cinemagraphic dubbing.

Over the years, I wondered why my European friends and colleagues, especially Spaniards, Italians, and Greeks, spoke the language of Shakespeare with such strong accents. Perhaps the problem—if it was a problem—was accentuated by the contrast I heard when Latin Americans spoke English—an English that, while not necessarily syntactically correct or complete in vocabulary, was infinitely more faithful as far as accent and the difficult pronunciation were concerned. For example, it was simple to identify a Spaniard speaking English but difficult to tell the difference between an Argentine or a Colombian communicating in that same tongue.

For a while I thought this singularity must be related to the way English is taught in each country, or in the physical characteristics of our mouths, tongues, and bodies as we speak our native language. Later on, I learned that the matter is much simpler but no less surprising. The key to the way we pronounce English lies in the fact that in Europe, movies are dubbed into local languages, while in Latin America, American and British movies have subtitles. Accustomed since childhood to hearing and seeing at the same time, we *latinoamericanos* learned English by listening, assimilating its inflections, sometimes like Robert De Niro in *The Godfather*, other times in the British English of James Ivory or Anthony Hopkins. Of course, we had to study its grammar and vocabulary, but above all we *heard* it, we took on its various cadences thanks to the big screen, a privilege denied to anyone who grew up with dubbed movies. Here perhaps is one of the few advantages of being so far from God and so close to the United States.

The result of this phenomenon is the good fortune of our prosodic standardization, the neutral way we Latin Americans speak English, which is not at all Latin, nor American, nor British, nor Australian or Irish, for example. This confirms the notion that English now belongs to those who speak it as a second language, the way American or British English have become mere dialects of a universal and neutral language that owes less to its origins every day.

In my own case, the experience of hearing English was itself subjected to a number of culture shocks. I spent my early days in a bilingual American school, then I studied English for years in a rigorously British academy. Later I survived in that language for the first time at a multiracial school in South Africa, where the native accent was so dissimilar that sometimes they made me believe I spoke anything but English. As if that were not enough, destiny has brought me to Scotland and England, and each time my vocabulary and pronunciation have suffered authentic shocks, to which are added the impact of having studied Italian, German, Dutch, French, and Portuguese. I believe the result could not be more representative of our times: a strange English which makes my English-speaking friends hesitate, an English which makes me pass as French or Israeli, never Latino. Naturally, the constant mutability of my accent has led to a permanent invention of grammar and words that appear English and in some way are English. But at this point, the only thing I can say is that I speak English as if I wore a mask made of masks.

IGNACIO PADILLA (Mexico City, Mexico; 1968-) is the well-traveled author of *Shadow without a Name,* the short story collection *Antipodes,* and *La catedral de los ahogados,* which won the Juan Rulfo Prize for first novel. Padilla has served as his nation's cultural attaché in London. In 2006 he was named director of Mexico's national library.

Writing in Between

— ROSARIO FERRÉ —

SOME TIME AGO I read that newborn babies suck faster at the breast if they hear someone speak their mother's language, which they learn to recognize in the womb. I did not begin to speak English until I was seven, and I learned most of it from books. By ten I had read *Wuthering Heights, Jane Eyre, The Three Musketeers,* and *The Thousand and One Nights* by sneaking into my family's library. I speak English with a Spanish accent; *canary* and *cannery* make me tremble when I have to say them because my pronunciation often gets me into trouble. Spanish still makes me suck faster at life's breast.

I write Spanish the way I speak it. Fast. For me, Spanish is "*la lengua escrita*"; English is "the written word." That's why it's impossible for me to write in English the same way I write in Spanish. English makes me slow down. I have to think about what I'm going to say two or three times—which may be good, as that way I can't put my foot, or rather my pen, in it so easily. I can't be trigger-happy in English, because words take too much effort.

How does one write the tongue, *la lengua*, in English? Contrary to English, Spanish literature has an oral quality to it, and Caribbean literature especially so, since it comes from an oral tradition. Caribbean stories are like incantations; their meaning often cannot be discerned until they are read out loud. In English the written word has Milton, Shakespeare, and the King James Version of the Bible standing behind it, swords drawn. In Spanish *la lengua escrita* doesn't have to be taken so seriously; there's more room in it for *bachata* and *relajo*, for irreverent humor and word play.

To say it in plain English, I love to write in Spanish. Spanish is like an exuberant jungle I love to get lost in, meandering down paths of words that often don't lead anywhere but to the rustle of their own foliage. Like Rocinante, Don Quijote's horse, I can roll on the ground and frolic in Spanish because I don't have to worry about anything—words always mean exactly what they say. I love to make love in Spanish; I've never been able to make love in English. In English I get puritanical; I could never do a belly dance, dance a Flamenco, or do a *zapateao* in English.

Writing in English is like looking at the world through a different pair of binoculars; it imposes a different mind-set. When I write in Spanish, my sentences are often as convoluted as a baroque *retablo*. When I write in English, Locke is locked into every sentence. Each paragraph has to be like a beam placed across the ceiling, to be covered with bricks of meaning. In English I have to be precise as well as practical. I feel like Emily Dickinson with a "loaded gun" in my hand; if I shoot, I have to take serious aim and try to bring down my target. Otherwise I know I'm going to get shot at.

Perhaps because I learned English by reading it, I write in it to be read, not to be listened to. When I was in elementary school I was taught that English was the language of the disciplined, orderly, hard-working *norteamericanos* who landed at Guánica in 1898. The americanos came to civilize us, to teach us how to behave and to control our Latin temper. So, when I write in English, I immediately stop being a gushing Romantic, an impractical poet, a lazy Puerto Rican who gives her books away to her friends, loves to go barefoot, and is still a savage at heart, and become a hard nosed, disciplined writer who wants to sell her books to the americanos and make money.

And yet beneath my Puerto Rican English a Latino passion throbs, a salsa rhythm swings. I like to be coming and going from English to Spanish and from Spanish to English, from the conga drums to the violins. Language has become *la guagua aérea* for me, an air bus, for it keeps me flying *entre* Puerto Rico and New York.

Puerto Rican writers write in Spanish. Our books are seldom translated into English and few of them are known in the United

States. Nor does our literature commonly reach Latin American countries, in spite of the shared language. For almost a hundred years we have inhabited a cultural no-man's-land. In Latin America we are considered milk-fed gringos; in North America we are greasy spiks. This ambivalence has contributed to our isolation and to the limited distribution of our books off the island.

Nine decades ago, with the Jones Act, education in English was made mandatory in our schools, even though our vernacular was Spanish. We tried to erase Spanish from our tongues. Puerto Ricans, we were told by Spanish professors at universities in the States, didn't really speak Spanish. We spoke a patois that everyone understood in Spain. Mexicans spoke Tapatío Spanish, Argentines spoke Bonaerense Spanish, but we Boricuas spoke *a lengua de mapo* Spanish, *como el superintendente del* building. We became ashamed of our tongue and were afraid to use it. Whenever *latinomericanos* got together in public forums everyone spoke Spanish *hasta por los codos*, up to their elbows, but we stumbled and struggled, completely tongue-tied.

When the Americans arrived in Puerto Rico in 1898, we were one of the poorest countries of the Third World, and we were overwhelmed by a feeling of inadequacy. We were invaded by consumer goods that we'd never seen before and didn't have names for in Spanish. They stood on our shelves like mysterious objects: canned Boston baked beans, electric fans, toothbrushes. *Los Boricuas* became *los mudos*, mute: we didn't know English and had forgotten Spanish.

Learning English *a la trágala*, by force, wasn't a matter of learning a second language; it was a matter of giving up one language for another. Of course it didn't work. From the moment we were compelled to speak English, we refused to learn it. People laughed at English; it was the language of those who saw themselves as superior to us and weren't; the tongue of *los Estados Fundillos*, who thought we couldn't govern ourselves and had turned us into a protectorate; the tongue of Chicago, which had two expletives in it, "cago" and "shit." It wasn't until the forties, when hundreds of thousands of Puerto Ricans emigrated to the States, that English began to trickle down our collective unconscious. Today, when 2.5 million Puerto Ricans live coming and going from the United States, the trickle has become a flood. In spite of being lazy Puerto Ricans, we finally picked up Bronx and Chicago English.

Why is it so difficult for Americans to learn Spanish? Below the Río Grande, millions are speaking Spanish and Portuguese, we are neighbors and need each other to survive. The United States thinks it's the navel of the world and doesn't need to pick up anyone else's tongue. To have a second tongue is suspect; *double-tongued* is a deprecatory term. And yet it's important for Americans to learn other languages; it's the reasonable, practical thing to do, as well as the most humane. It's ironic that the United States, with its enormous cultural influence and economic power, often behaves like an island with the rest of the world.

To speak more than one language is typical of the Caribbean. Puerto Ricans are typically Caribbean: we speak Spanish and English. Other islanders such as Jamaicans speak English, Patois, Chinese; Trinidadians also speaks many languages. Each time Caribbeans return from the States they bring back a crumb, a flake, a nugget of gold from its citadels. These are islands literally floating "in between" North and South America. And yet, I refuse to see this as a peril; multilingualism can be a tremendous advantage. I see no reason to give up one language if I can help it. "*Más vale un diente que un diamante, Sancho, amigo,*" Don Quijote said. "A language is worth more than a diamond." And the same can be said of biculturalism. We should be able to speak not just two but three or four languages. As a Puerto Rican I can write from both sides of the arrow, Spanish and English, aimed at the same target: understanding.

ROSARIO FERRÉ (Ponce, Puerto Rico; 1938-), recipient of a Guggenheim Fellowship, is the author of *Flight of the Swan, Sweet Diamond Dust,* and *The House on the Lagoon,* a finalist for the National Book Award. She has also authored children's books and a newspaper column of literary criticism as well as a biography of her father, Luis, a highly regarded *puertorriqueño* active in politics, the arts, and business.

Pink Floyd
Taught Me English

— ROBERTO QUESADA —

I WAS RAISED in Honduras and developed my literary vocation with the help of my beloved stepfather, José Adán Castelar, a poet of the Left. He opposed U.S. policy toward Latin America, especially during the Cold War, and agreed with the great Portuguese novelist José María Eca de Queiroz, who said, "The patriot should speak foreign languages badly."

Thanks to his left-wing dogmatism, I grew up estranged from anything that smelled of the United States, and was more familiar with Russian classics and language. In fact, the Soviet Union was good, and anything having to do with the United States was bad. In retrospect I can see that these terrible divisions caused by ideology, religion, and the urge to dominate confirm that humanity is still in its infancy. Of course, all this made my encounter with English and U.S. culture that much more traumatic.

That encounter began with a girl, Aída Sabonge, a Honduran who grew up in New Orleans and returned to Honduras, where we got married. She taught English at the Autonomous National University of Honduras, and on occasion we visited her colleagues at their homes. It bothered me that even though we were nearly all Hondurans, they usually spoke English. I was frustrated at not understanding, and sometimes I became paranoid, convinced that they were talking about me. Instead of learning English, I resisted the language of Shakespeare.

Later we visited New Orleans. There I saw another side of the United States. For the first time, I heard jazz, which I had known only through the writings of Argentine author Julio Cortázar. I read Walker Percy, John Kennedy Toole, and others in Spanish translations. Of course, I had read Faulkner, Whitman, Poe, and Hemingway, but I considered them universal, not specifically North American.

Editor Dan Simon invited me to be part of a reading of Central American stories at Cooper Union in New York City. He had to pay not only for me but also for my wife, since she was my interpreter. The reading would be bilingual.

There the writers gathered behind the scenes, most of us Latinos. I saw a tall man with a big mustache, wearing jeans and a dark blue shirt, standing by himself. I felt sorry for him and approached so he wouldn't feel alone. He did not speak one word of Spanish and I spoke no English, but he was pleased with my efforts and we had good chemistry. It was February 1989 and very cold. I showed him the bottle of Jack Daniel's I carried under my jacket and we looked for a couple of plastic cups. Inspired by the whiskey, we began a wonderful mute conversation.

There we were, laughing, perhaps at one another or at ourselves. Suddenly Aída appeared. She was startled and greeted him with deference. Then she asked me, "Do you know who he is?" I replied, "A poor gringo who's marginalized for not speaking Spanish." She laughed at me, pitying my ignorance, and said, "He is the great writer Kurt Vonnegut, the Gabriel García Márquez of the United States."

She began to interpret. I had understood his name as Karl, as in Karl Marx, and not Kurt. I showed him the Spanish version of my novel, Los barcos—The Ships—and tried to tell him it was about to be translated into English. He thought I had told him it was the Central American best-seller. And then we laughed because we had understood nothing.

Then came the lecture. Vonnegut liked the excerpt I read from my novel and I asked for his address so I could send him the translation. Two months later I returned, without my wife, to live in New York. I had found work managing a Central American community newspaper. I noted the profound difference between New Orleans and New York accents and felt like I was part of Woody Allen's *The Purple Rose of Cairo*. I found Vonnegut's address and phone number and practiced saying: "Hello, Mr. Vonnegut… I'm Roberto, the Honduran writer… You remember me?" Finally I mustered the courage to call him. I said "Hello," and to this day I don't know what he said, but I responded "Yes" to everything.

Shortly after I arrived in New York, Dan Shapiro, who later became the literature director of the Americas Society, introduced me to a young blonde and served as Cupid by interpreting our initial conversation. She invited me to her apartment a few days later.

The blonde spoke no Spanish and I no English. We had dinner. We made love. We sat down in the living room and she said, "Roberto, talk to me." I tried to understand her simple words, and we made love again. Later she said again, "Roberto, talk to me." Same result. Afterward she repeated the same sentence: "Roberto, talk to me." I figured she was either crazy or a nymphomaniac and I remembered strange stories about what happens in big cities. Since I didn't speak English, I tried to use logic. When I bought cigarettes on the street, I always got a little book of matches with cheesy photos of naked ladies that said, "Talk to me." I thought that "talk" meant *talco*, which also meant "powder" in Spanish. And then I translated "to me" correctly as *a mí*. Since in slang *powder* meant "to have sex," I translated "talk to me" as *cógeme* (screw me). I never saw that blonde again.

I had seen Pink Floyd's movie The *Wall* and loved it. To practice my English I watched it over and over just to say the words aloud and adapt my tongue to Shakespeare's language. When I was next in Honduras I showed it to some friends. It was only as we sat down to look at it that I realized it had no subtitles; I was thrilled to be able to interpret it. Luckily I knew it by heart.

Later I became friends with the denizens of the Nuyorican Poet Café on New York's Lower East Side. Miguel Algarín, a founder of the Café, always embarrassed me by correcting me in a loud voice, but I learned from his criticisms. The late poet and playwright Pedro Pietri, on the other hand, spoke to me softly in Spanglish. That was my school: friends, bars, visits to cultural centers.

I was soon asked to translate a biography of Gloria Estefan. I knew translation was serious business through my friendship with two masters of the form: Hardie St. Martin, who would translate my novel *Los barcos* into English, and Gregory Rabassa, who translated García Márquez's *One Hundred Years of Solitude* and Cortázar's *Rayuela*, among others. They convinced me that translation is an art.

At first I felt incapable, but I needed the money and took on the challenge, come what may. I spent more than a month, barely sleeping or leaving the house, but I did it. Of course, translating a biography written in English is not the same as translating poetry or fiction.

I began learning English when I arrived in New York simply by listening and asking questions. Some needs were so pressing they compelled me to speak English. One friend made me see the film *West Side Story*, perhaps more for the action than for the music. Whatever her motive, watching the Jets battle the Sharks over and over brought me closer to English.

I never took formal English classes. I taught myself instead, with all kinds of books including dictionaries of both conventional and slang English. I reread novels in English that I already knew in Spanish. I often heard people cite the *New York Times* when they talked about politics, so I subscribed. Within two months I could read it easily.

My great English classroom has been, and continues to be, life in New York City.

ROBERTO QUESADA (Olanchito, Honduras; 1962-) is the author of the novels *The Big Banana*, *The Ships*, and *Never through Miami*. His short stories have appeared in Germany, Russia, Spain, and Great Britain. An occasional lecturer on American campuses, Quesada serves as counselor of the Honduran Mission to the United Nations.

The Trouble with English

– GLORIA LÓPEZ–STAFFORD –

Excerpted from *My Place in El Paso: A Mexican American Childhood*

IN THE SEGUNDO BARRIO during the 1940s, people spoke Spanish. They spoke the Spanish they brought with them from their ranchos, villages, and cities. They also brought the music of their accents. You could tell by the quality of their speech whether they were country or city people. Spanish in the 1940s in South El Paso was formal and polite. People apologized if they said a word like *estúpido*. I would often wonder why that required an apology. And I would be told that people from rural areas are not open with criticism and do not want to offend with what they consider vulgar language.

When people left the barrio, they began using English more. You still spoke Spanish at home because that was what your family used. Then when you spoke with someone who also spoke both languages, the language evolved to a mixture of English and Spanish that became an art form. Sometimes sentences might be in one language with certain words in the other. Other times whole paragraphs might be in one language and only a few sentences in the other. It was a living language, a musical score that conveyed the optimal sense, meaning, and feeling from both languages that a single language might not achieve. The combination drew criticism from purists and people who did not speak both. They accused the bilingual person of being lazy or undisciplined. But I think it was a love for both languages that made it impossible to be faithful to just one. On the other hand, cussing or profanity were best in English. The words were just words to me. Cussing in Spanish was painful and created emotions that led to guilt. And, it was unacceptable to our parents and priests....

At least once a week [my father] Palm and I would have a talk about why I wasn't learning English. I saw no reason to. I had to experience a need for it, and that is what happened.

"You have to learn English, Gloria," Palm would say.

"I don't want to. I don't have to. I don't need it," I would stubbornly refuse.

"I suppose you didn't need it at the border on Saturday when immigration held you after you were in Juárez with López and you couldn't answer their questions?" he said firmly. "I had to leave the store to go and get them to release you. All because you can't carry on a conversation in English."

I had created problems for Palm and myself, but I didn't want to learn English and that was that.

On this particular morning, I waited for Palm to get tired of the topic and to move on to something else. But he didn't. He continued.

"The note the teacher sent home says that you will not speak English. She says that everyone speaks for you. And she says that you talk all the time, but in Spanish! It's been a month since school started and she says you will not cooperate. She says she is going to have to punish you. She wrote to inform me that she is at the end of her patience with you," Palm said.

"So that is what the *mugre* [dirty] note said. I thought she liked me," I said as I thought of how she and I grinned at each other every day. I didn't understand what she was saying and she didn't know what I was saying. She could have been speaking Chinese just like the Chinos near the Cuauhtemoc market in Juárez. I just didn't want to speak English.

"It sounds ugly. And I look stupid speaking it," I admitted when I saw the look on Palm's face.

"It's because you don't use it enough to get used to it," Palm tried to explain.

"My friends and I don't need to speak it. We have our own way of speaking." I continued the argument until I noticed that Palm was frustrated and quiet. I decided to play. I put my left hand on my hip and shook my right index finger menacingly.

"Wo do bo to do ri ra do fo, da mo, meeester!" I said in gibberish. "Ha, no, meeezter?" I raised my eyebrow and looked at Palm. "That's English!"

"Payasa. You are very stubborn. You need to learn English." Palm started up again. "My son is coming to visit and he speaks English."

The last remark caught my attention. I turned my eyes to the picture of Palm's son, which was displayed in a large oval frame. He resembled Palm. I wondered why he was only my half brother. When I was younger, I thought it was because only the upper part of his body was in the picture. Palm corrected me. He told me his son had a different mother and was the only one of his children that stayed in touch with him. He loved Palm very much and would write to him every week. He was the youngest child and had been in college when my father went to Mexico. Palm's son's light eyes seemed to follow me around the room.

Palm was still talking about a visit from his son when I found my voice and said, "*¡Que suave!* When he comes, I'll tell him all about me and the neighborhood." Palm just nodded his head and gave me a strange look.

The next week, when I got home from school, I was frightened because I thought someone was in the apartment. But Palm called to me when I pressed my nose against the screen to look inside.

"*Entra, mi'ja.*" Palm's voice was happy. I pulled the screen door open and entered the living room. A man was with my father. He looked like my father, but he wasn't old; he looked familiar. Then, suddenly, my eyes turned to the picture on the wall. I looked at the man and I looked at the picture. They were the same!

"*¡Hola! ¿Cómo estás?*" I yelled with happiness as I ran to hug the stranger. He returned the hug. I was overjoyed. Palm was telling the truth about his son coming to visit. Here he was… all of him!

Palm's son opened his mouth and said something to Palm who was telling him something too. They were speaking Chinese!

"Papá, tell him that I speak Spanish," I told my father.

"Yoya, he knows." Palm spoke slowly because he knew how I would react. "He doesn't speak Spanish. He only speaks English. I told you many times."

I was speechless. What a dirty *trampa* (trick)!

"Didn't you tell him I didn't speak English? Did you forget?" I questioned my Palm as the other Palm looked on with the biggest and sweetest smile. How could he not speak Spanish? I started to cry, but the other Palm understood as my father told him in Chinese what the problem was. Palm's son laughed as he picked me up and kissed me as he said something to my father. I looked to Palm for a translation.

"He says you're as precious as he knew you would be. He's sorry that he can't speak Spanish. He has never been able to learn," my father said.

I hugged his son and just watched them as they talked. Occasionally, Palm would tell me what they were saying if he thought it might interest me. I just kept looking into our visitor's beautiful face. My little chest was heavy with the weight of my broken heart. I had so wanted to be able to talk with him. I couldn't believe it. And I knew Palm had warned me.

When the sunset, the color of West Texas sweet potato flesh, began to spread across the barrio, our visitor said he had to leave. We went outside. Palm's son picked me up and kissed me. Palm softly told me what his son was saying to me.

"He says he loves you, Yoya. He hopes that when you meet again, either you'll know English or he'll know Spanish."

I hugged and kissed my favorite visitor back. It would be many years before I would see him again and it would be long after our father's death. But on this evening, my father and I watched him as he walked to Virginia Street where he had parked his car. Palm and I sat on the cement step. As the car pulled off with my half–brother, I turned to Palm and said with determination and sadness, "It's time I learned English, Papi."

"*Sí, corazón*, yes." He understood.

GLORIA LÓPEZ-STAFFORD (Ciudad Juárez, Mexico; 1937-) is the author of the memoir *A Place in El Paso: A Mexican American Childhood,* which tells of innocence and turmoil in the author's life and that of El Paso. López-Stafford, who worked for the Gadsden Independent School District in the part of New Mexico that adjoins El Paso, was a professor of social work and is now retired.

My Cuban Parents Learn English in Night School

– VIRGIL SUÁREZ –

to, two, too
there, their, they're

two to tango
factory work

yeses & noses
picky bosses

piecemeal work
conjunctions, verbs,

prepositions
"C" is for Capitalism,

compounds of colors:
fuchsia, ambrosia

ochre hearth
flies in the buttermilk

shoofly's shoes
cheaper, faster

hocus-pocus
faster, cheaper

heebie-jeebies
everyday of the week

repeat after me
hard work, hard work

crows the raven:
speak English

VIRGIL SUÁREZ (Havana, Cuba; 1962-) is the widely anthologized author of many books of poetry (*In the Republic of Longing, 90 Miles,* and *Palm Crows*), short stories (*Welcome to the Oasis*), novels (*Going Under, Latin Jazz,* and *The Cutter*), and memoir (*Infinite Refuge* and *Spared Angola*). He has also served as co-editor of collections of Latino literature. His many distinctions include a grant from the National Endowment for the Arts and the Latino Literature Hall of Fame Poetry Prize. Suárez teaches in the creative writing program at Florida State University in Tallahassee.

English Is Cuh-ray-zee

– RICHARD LEDERER & JOSH WHITE JR. –

ENGLISH IS THE MOST widely spoken language in the history of
the planet.
One out of every seven human beings can speak or read it.
Half the world's books, 3/4 of the international mail is in English.
It has the largest vocabulary, perhaps two million words,
And a noble body of literature. But face it:
English is cuh-ray-zee!

Just a few examples: There's no egg in eggplant, no pine or apple
in pineapple.
Quicksand works slowly; boxing rings are square.
A writer writes, but do fingers fing?
Hammers don't ham, grocers don't groce. Haberdashers don't
haberdash.
English is cuh-ray-zee!

If the plural of tooth is teeth, shouldn't the plural of booth be beeth?
It's one goose, two geese. Why not one moose, two meese?
If it's one index, two indices; why not one Kleenex, two Kleenices?
English is cuh-ray-zee!

You can comb through the annals of history, but not just one annal.
You can make amends, but not just one amend.
If you have a bunch of odds and ends and get rid of all but one, is
it an odd or an end?
If the teacher taught, why isn't it true that a preacher praught?
If you wrote a letter, did you also bote your tongue?

And if a vegetarian eats vegetables, what does a humanitarian eat?
English is cuh-ray-zee!

Why is it that night falls but never breaks and day breaks but
   never falls?
In what other language do people drive on the parkway and park
   on the driveway?
Ship by truck but send cargo by ship? Recite at a play but play at a
   recital?
Have noses that run and feet that smell?
English is cuh-ray-zee!
How can a slim chance and a fat chance be the same
When a wise man and a wise guy are very different?
To overlook something and to oversee something are very different,
But quite a lot and quite a few are the same.
How can the weather be hot as hell one day and cold as hell the next?
English is cuh-ray-zee!

You have to marvel at the lunacy of a language in which your
   house can burn down
While it is burning up. You fill out a form by filling it in.
In which your alarm clock goes off by going on.
If pro is the opposite of con, what is the opposite of progress?
English is cuh-ray-zee!

Well, English was invented by people, not computers
And reflects the creativity of the human race.
So that's why when the stars are out, they're visible,
But when the lights are out, they're invisible.
When I wind up my watch I start it, but when I wind up this rap,
I end it. English is cuh-ray-zee!

RICHARD LEDERER is an author and commentator on the English language and its endless idiosyncrasies. JOSH WHITE JR. is a star
of stage, television, recordings, and concert performances.

AFTERWORD

— BY FRANK McCOURT —

THIS IS A THANK-YOU note to the English for imposing their language on my Irish ancestors eight hundred years ago. Otherwise I might be writing this afterword in Irish or Gaelic or Erse and who among you would be capable of reading it?

In primary school in Ireland we were told how our ancestors bravely resisted the invading English, who were actually Norman and French-speaking. It was hard for us kids to get this straight. English? French? What in God's name did those invaders speak and how did they force our noble ancestors to speak their language? (We were told, also, that English was an ugly language—a set of brays, hisses, and grunts.)

The English fought the Normans. The Normans fought the English. They both fought the Irish, but everyone bowed to the other language going the rounds at the time: Latin. That was the language of scholarship and religion, and it behooved you to bend a knee to the priest who spoke it at the altar.

Our ancestors were noble. No doubt about that. They never surrendered completely and all through those eight centuries they fought for their language—so sparkling and musical. We learned that many of those English/Norman invaders became more Irish than the Irish themselves and even took to the language of the native. Who could resist those dimpled colleens going about their business and singing in the native tongue the most beautiful stories of love? Who?

All this was illuminating and entertaining, but I often cursed my ancestors who kept Irish alive.

And this is why I cursed:

A little biographical information might be helpful here. I was born in New York, where I lisped English as my first language. When I was four, my parents returned to Ireland and in a few weeks put me in primary school.

I have a vivid memory of that first class. There was the schoolmaster, Mr. Tom Scanlon, pointing with a stick at something on the blackboard and roaring at the kids: "This is the Irish alphabet. This is what your forefathers fought and died for." (No matter what subject you studied in school then, you were told someone had died for it.) Letter by letter, we chanted the Irish alphabet. Then Mr. Scanlon picked on us, individually, to recite certain letters, and if we mispronounced them he whacked us across the shoulders with his stick and told us we should thank the living God we had our own language when millions around the world were deprived of theirs. "Look at the Americans. Gangsters and cowboys. Sure, they hardly know what they're saying at all, at all."

In the matter of Irish, some masters were more fanatical than others. We were grateful when we discovered in third grade that Mr. Bob Cashin seemed indifferent to the language our ancestors had fought and died for. He told us the mother of all languages was Latin and if a man knew no Latin, he was an ignoramus and barely Christian, to boot.

Mr. O'Dea, in fifth grade, was an Irish fanatic. If he had had his way, English would have been banned entirely. He applied Irish at the end of a stick and we came to hate the language so much we swore we'd never utter a word of it when we left school.

But now, decades later, I feel sad at the thought that Gaelic/Irish is a dying language. The government tries to prop it up by pouring money into Irish-speaking communities on the country's west coast. Unless young rock stars like Sinead O'Connor sing in the ancient language it is bound to disappear.

When I returned to New York at 19, I was happy to be able to speak English and often wondered what life would have been like if I knew only Gaelic. Like the writers in this book, I would have had to struggle with a new language and that, as the writers know, is hard when you also have to make your way in a new culture. As a high school English teacher, I witnessed those daily struggles with language. I saw teenagers who wanted to be American and cool vent their frustrations, sometimes in violence, but more often in clownish posturing. I was frustrated myself when I was assigned to teach English as a Second Language. I fumbled through a year of this and the only thing that saved me was that the kids understood that, like them, I came from another country. They didn't understand that English was my first language. I let them think we were all in the same boat.

This book, *How I Learned English*, triggers hundreds of memories for me, though I hope there were no kids in my classes like Josefina López who writes here of her suffering and embarrassment when an uncomprehending teacher refused her the bathroom pass. When Josefina pees in her pants a teacher assistant says, "You should have said you *really* had to go."

This is a book of high linguistic adventure and it's bound to lead to reflection on the lives of people in our own time who slip across our borders. Politics aside, you can only admire the millions who came here and are still coming, who climb the highest mountain of all—the English language.

FRANK McCOURT is the author of the best-selling *Angela's Ashes*, *'Tis*, and *Teacher Man*.

TRANSLATORS

WHY, IF THIS BOOK DEALS with learning English, did I invite contributors to send in their pieces in Spanish if they wished? Easy. Just because you have acquired a second language doesn't mean your writing is as subtle, clever, emotional, or fluid as it is in your first. I wanted the best these people could offer, and if reaching back to their youths and emotional turning points demanded their first language, then I was happy to have their impressions in Spanish.

I was fortunate to engage the services of some outstanding translators, interpreters of the written word who took into account a country's vocabulary, everyday slang, and individual voice. One contributor asked me to employ her husband, who translates all her work; another had a colleague at her college translate her piece. Both made wise decisions. Translators perform magic, achieving the almost impossible task of making the second language read as smoothly as the first. These are the magicians:

George Evans translated Daisy Zamora's contribution.

Nancy Hand translated pieces by Lorena Ochoa and Miguel Barnet.

Beth Henson was the translator for Ignacio Padilla, Gabriel Trujillo Muñoz, and Roberto Quesada.

Barbara Leblanc, working with Ray Faith, translated the piece by Teresa Méndez-Faith.

Lauren McElroy Herrera translated essays by Paquito D'Rivera, José Kozer, and Germán Arciniegas.

Kelley Merriam Castro translated contributions from Mayra Montero and Jesús Vega.

Annamarie Schaecher translated the piece by Mario Kreutzberger ("Don Francisco").

—T.M.

COPYRIGHTS/ PERMISSIONS

ABOUT THE EDITOR

JAY ROCHLIN

TOM MILLER (Washington, D.C.; 1947-), who conceived and edited this volume, has been bringing us extraordinary stories of ordinary people for more than 30 years. His highly acclaimed travel books include *The Panama Hat Trail*, about South America; *On the Border*, an account of his adventures in the U.S.-Mexico frontier; *Trading with the Enemy*, which takes readers on his journeys through Cuba; and *Jack Ruby's Kitchen Sink* about the American Southwest, which won the Lowell Thomas Award for Best Travel Book of 2000. Additionally, he has edited two collections: *Travelers' Tales—Cuba* and *Writing on the Edge: A Borderlands Reader*. His articles have appeared in *Smithsonian*, the *New Yorker*, the *New York Times*, *Life*, *Natural History*, and many other publications. He lives in Arizona. More about Mr. Miller may be found at www.tommillerbooks.com. This is his tenth book.